Friggin' Bean Counters

Navigating the BS infested cubicles of the Accounting department

Written by Karla Sasser • Illustrated by Gary Solomon

Published by: KSasser, PL

Friggin' Bean Counters: Navigating the BS infested cubicles of the Accounting department

Published by: **KSasser, PL, Fruitland Park, FL**

Copyright © 2014 by KSasser, PL

No part of the publication may be reproduced, stored in a retrieval system or transmitted in any form or by any means, electronic, mechanical, photocopying, recording, scanning, printing or otherwise, except as permitted under Sections 107 or 108 of the 1976 United States Copyright Act, without either the prior written permission of the Publisher, or authorization through payment of the appropriate per copy fee to the Copyright Clearance Center, 222 Rosewood Drive, Danvers, MA 01923. Request to the Publisher for permission should be emailed to frigginbeancounter@accountant.com.

LIMIT OF LIABILITY / DISCLAIMER OF WARRANTY: THE PUBLISHER AND AUTHOR MAKE NO REPRESENTATIONS OR WARRANTIES WITH RESPECT TO THE ACCURACY OR COMPLETENESS OF THE CONTENTS OF THIS WORK. SPECIFICALLY ALL WARRANTIES, INCLUDING WITHOUT LIMITATION WARRANTIES OF FITNESS FOR A PARTICULAR PURPOSE ARE DISCLAIMED. NO WARRANTIES MAYBE CREATED OR EXTENDED BY SALES OR PROMOTIONAL MATERIALS. THE ADVICE AND STRATEGIES CONTAINED IN THIS WORK MAY NOT BE SUITABLE FOR EVERY SITUATION. THIS WORKS IS SOLD WITH THE UNDERSTANDING THAT THE PUBLISHER IS NOT ENGAGED IN GIVING LEGAL, ACCOUNTING OR OTHER PROFESSIONAL SERVICES. IF PROFESSIONAL SERVICES ARE REQUIRED, A COMPETENT PROFESSIONAL PERSON OR FIRM SHOULD BE ENGAGED. NEITHER THE PUBLISHER NOR THE AUTHOR SHALL BE LIABLE FOR DAMAGES ARISING FROM THE USE OF THIS WORK. ORGANIZATIONS OR WEBSITES REFERRED TO IN THIS WORK AS A CITATION AND/OR POTENTIAL SOURCE OF FURTHER INFORMATION DOES NOT CONSTITUTE ENDORSEMENT BY THE PUBLISHER OR THE AUTHOR. READERS SHOULD BE AWARE THAT INTERNET WEBSITES CITED IN THIS WORK MY CHANGE OR DISAPPEAR BETWEEN THE WRITING AND PUBLICATION OF THIS WORK.

For information regarding the publication please email

frigginbeancounter@accountant.com

Library of Congress Registration Number: TXu 2-003-594

ISBN 978-0-9907637-0-3

ACKNOWLEDGMENTS AND DEDICATIONS

With great appreciation -

I would like to thank John R. Alexander and the Association of Chartered Accountants in the United States for much of the information presented in the first three chapters. Excerpts were taken from *History of Accounting,* courtesy of the publisher. Without knowing how it all started, understanding where we are and how we got here is impossible.

I would also like to thank my colleagues, Sonia Luna, CPA, and Amit Dewan, CPA, for providing me with the flexibility and freedom to complete this project.

This book is dedicated to each person who has touched my life as a result of both the good and bad life choices I have made. Most of all to my husband, whose unwavering love and belief in me has been my constant support and encouragement.

Written by: Karla Sasser

Illustrated by: Gary Solomon

Edited by: Caitlin Houston

Technical/Peer Review by
Sonia Luna, CPA; Amit Dewan, CPA;
Norachai Chawareewong, CPA; Len Wood, CPA

TABLE OF CONTENTS

Table of Figures, Illustrations, Pictures, Tables & Charts vii

Introduction 1

Chapter 1 - Friggin' Bean Counters - Came From Nowhere to Make Life Miserable 11

    3150 BC - 30 BC: Mesopotamia and Ancient Egypt 12

    500 BC - 401 BC: Classical Greece 15

    27 BC - 14 AD: Ancient Rome 16

    15 BC - 1300 AD: Medieval Accounting 17

    1301 AD - 1600 AD: Italian Renaissance 19

Chapter 2 - Friggin' Bean Counters - Stole Our Computers 23

    1601 AD - 1700 AD: Europe's Early Modern Period 24

    1801 AD - 1900 AD: The 19th Century and the Industrial Revolutions 26

    Birth of the Accounting Profession 26

    Visionaries begin the Computer Evolution! 28

    The Accounting Profession Moves to the United States! 30

    1901 - 1939 the Computer Evolution Begins! 32

    1940 - 1956: First Generation Computers 33

    1956 - 1963: Second Generation Computers 36

    1964 - 1971: Third Generation Computers 37

    1971 - NOW: Fourth Generation Computers 38

    NOW and Beyond: Fifth Generation Computers 38

    How is the Evolution of Computers Related to Accounting? 38

Chapter 3 - Friggin' Bean Counters - Keep Your Rules 41

    Old Rules Never Change: They Just Get More Restrictive 42

    Wait, Didn't You Say the AICPA Was the Accounting Oversight? 44

    Who Makes the Rules? 46

Chapter 4 - Friggin' Bean Counters - Who Cares What the Numbers Are? 51

    Every Business Entity Needs to Count Beans 53

    Decision Makers Rely on Bean Counters 54

Chapter 5 - Friggin' Bean Counters - Finance or Accounting: Who Cares 57

    The Places Beans Are Counted - Typical Finance Functions within a Business 59

    More Places Where Beans Are Counted - Typical Accounting Functions within a Business 60

Chapter 6 - Friggin' Bean Counters - Isn't It All Counting Beans? 63

Chapter 7 - Friggin' Bean Counters - Who Needs 'Em? 67

    Meet the Bean Counters - The Accountants 68

Chapter 8 - Friggin' Bean Counters - Double Entry Double Talk 75

    The Many Essential Elements of the Bookkeeping System Needed to Count Beans 76

    To Keep the Bean Counts Accurate - Nine Steps of the Bookkeeping Cycle 78
    Counting the Beans for the Sales at Grandpa Otis' General Store 79

Chapter 9 - Friggin' Bean Counters - What Did You Do to Our Computers? 91

    Revenue Radicals or the Revenue Riot 92
    Understanding Revenue 92
    GAAP Rules for Proper Revenue Recognition 93
    IFRS & Revenue Recognition 103
    Expense Extremist - Understanding Expenses 105
    Unadjusted Trial Balance - Trial Balance on Trial 112

Chapter 10 - Friggin' Bean Counters - What's It Mean? Closing the Gap on GAAP 115

    Paper Clip Warehouse Financials 116

Chapter 11 - Friggin' Bean Counters - Manipulate and Misstate for Better Results? 127

    Financial Statement Manipulation and Misstatements 128
    Paper Clip Warehouse Manipulations 132

Chapter 12 - Friggin' Bean Counters - We Thought the Auditors Were Kind of Nerdy 139

    External Audits 140
    Generally Accepted Audit Standards 142
    Audit of the Paper Clip Warehouse 144
    Internal Audit Defined 147
    Internal Audit 149
    Systems Development Life Cycle 151

Chapter 13 - Friggin' Bean Counters - Control This! 153

Chapter 14 - Friggin' Bean Counters - We Are Not Going to Jail 167

    Securities Act of 1933 169
    Securities Exchange Act of 1934 169
    Foreign Corrupt Practices Act of 1977 170
    Transparency International 172
    Financial Services Modernization Act of 1999 172
    Sarbanes-Oxley Act of 2002 173
    Health Insurance Portability and Accountability Act of 1996 174
    Health Information Technology for Economic and Clinical Health Act of 2009 175
    The Bank Secrecy Act of 1970 and the U.S. Patriot Act of 2001 175
    Payment Card Industry Data Security Standards (PCIDSS) 176
    Office of Foreign Asset Control (OFAC) 177
    European Union Data Protection Directive of 1981 178
    Personal Information Protection and Electronic Documents Act of 1983 178
    Jumpstart Our Business Startups (JOBS) Act of 2012 179
    Why Is This Important? 179

Chapter 15 - Friggin' Bean Counters – Wrap It Up Please 181

    Satyam Computers Limited 183

Index 188

ENDNOTES 195

TABLE OF FIGURES, ILLUSTRATIONS, PICTURES, TABLES & CHARTS

Cuneiform Script – Source: Getty Images 13

Egyptian Scribe – Source: Personnelle de Gerard Ducher 14

Papyrus – Source: Wiki Commons 15

Classical Greek Coin – Source: Getty Images 15

Roman Coin - Source: Wiki Commons 16

William the Conqueror – Source: Bayeux Tapestry William Lifts His Helmet 17

Binding of the Doomsday Book - Source: Wiki Commons 18

CA 1459 German Manuscript – Source Wiki Commons 19

Blaise Pascal - Source: Wiki Commons 24

Pascaline Calculator (PASCAL 1642) - Source: Wiki Commons 25

Leibniz Wheel - Source: Purdue 25

Arithmometer - Source: Wiki Commons 27

Charles Xavier Thomas de Colmar - Source: Wiki Commons 27

Analytical Engine - Source: Wiki Commons 28

Charles Babbage - Source: Wiki Commons 28

Augusta Ada King - Source: Wiki Commons 28

Punch Card - Source: Wiki Commons 28

Tabulation Machine - Source: Wiki Commons 29

Herman Hollerith - Source: Wiki Commons 29

Vannevar Bush - Source: Wiki Commons 32

Differential Analyzer - Source: Wiki Commons 32

Howard Aiken - Source: Wiki Commons 33

ASCC – I/O Devices - Source: Wiki Commons 33

Eckert & Mauchly - Source: UNINA.STIDUE 34

ENIAC – Source: US Army 34

Vacuum Tubes – Source: Getty Images 34

Early Integrated Circuit by RCA - Source: Wiki Commons 35

Sir Maurice Vincent Wilkes - Source: Wiki Commons 35

William Shockley - Source: Wiki Commons 36

Geoffrey Dummer - Source: Wiki Commons 37

Robert Noyce - Source: Wiki Commons 37

Integrated Circuit - Source: Getty Images 38

1984 Macintosh by Apple - Source: Wiki Commons 38

Advertisement for the 8080 - Source: Wiki Commons 38

Code of Hammurabi - Source: Wiki Commons	42
Augustus of Prima Porta - Source: Wiki Commons	42
The Deeds - Source: Wiki Commons	43
Cover of Summa De Arithmetic - Source: Unknown	43
Portrait of Pacioli - Source: Wiki Commons	43
List of GAAP Standards – Source - ACCOUNTINGINFO.COM	46
TITLE 26 OF US LAW, Source: Office of the Law Revision Counsel	49
Basic Accounting Processes & How IT Fits In	55
Manual Bookkeeping Journals - Source: Wiki Commons	79
Grandpa Otis' POS System- Source: Getty Images	79
Ledger Paper, Grandma Otis' Spreadsheet - Source: Getty Images	81
Normal Account Balances	82
General Store Chat of Accounts in a Manual Bookkeeping System	83
Messy Ledger in a Manual Bookkeeping System - Source: Getty Images	84
Journal Entries Prepared by Grandma Otis	85
Technologies that Made the Automation of Bookkeeping Possible	87
The Manual Bookkeeping for the Sales Cycle	88
Accounting for Revenue under U.S. GAAP	95
Current and Future Paper Clip Warehouse Division	94
Departments within the Paper Clip Warehouse Divisions	94
Paper Clip Warehouse Chart of Accounts	96-98
Journal Entry Prepared by the Accounting Clerk	99
Basic Automated Journal Entry Process	99
Standard POS Transaction Codes for the Paper Clip Warehouse	100
Journal Entries for Transactions 3-6	101
Nightly Batch Processing Routine for Recording Sales	102
Journal Entry for Transactions 7	103
Accounting for Expenses under U.S. GAAP.	106
Basic Accounts Payable Process	107
Purchase Price Allocation	109
Payroll-Related Account Entries	112
Paper Clip Warehouse Unadjusted Trial Balance	113
Cost of Goods Sold Calculations	117
Allocation of Paper Clip Warehouse's Intangible Assets	117
Formula for Calculating Straight-Line Depreciation	118
Accounting for Paper Clip Warehouse Depreciation of Assets	118
Estimated Annual Property Taxes	119

Payroll Accrual for the Month of December 119

Interest Earned on the Marketable Securities 119

Amortization Table for the $10 Million Startup Loan 120

Consolidated Adjusted Trial Balance for the Paper Clip Warehouse 121

GAAP Based Paper Clip Warehouse Financial Statements 122-124

Basic Transaction Processing from Initiation to Inclusion on Financial Statements 125

Adjusted Balance Sheet for the Paper Clip Warehouse 134

Misstated Balance Sheet and Income Statement 136

Typical Debits and Credits for Specific Transactions 141

Trial Balance Provided to the Auditors 145

System Development Life Cycle - Source: Wiki Commons 151

We're Watching You - Source: Getty Images 168

SEC Act 1933 - Source: Getty Images 169

US SEC Commission – Source – U.S. Government 169

Bribes - Source: Getty Images 170

Corruption Index - Source: Wiki Commons 172

Modern Board Room - Source: Getty Images 172

SOX - Source: Getty Images 173

Healthcare - Source: Getty Images 174

Money Laundering - Source: Getty Images 175

U.S. Patriot Act - Source: Getty Images 176

Credit Card Thief - Source: Getty Images 176

PCI-DSS Requirements 176

Department of the Treasury - Source – U.S. Government 177

Data Thief – Source: Getty Images 178

INTRODUCTION

I have been a "friggin' bean counter" for many years and have spent a significant and rewarding portion of my career working for and with businesses in either accounting or internal audit management. I have worked for small businesses, non-profit healthcare organizations, and Fortune 1000 companies. Throughout my experiences, I have noticed two indisputable facts. First, Accounting is one of the largest departments of any organization and the largest consumer of company information technology (IT) resources and services. The second indisputable fact, unfortunately, is that Accounting and IT are generally at odds with one another. After many years of experience, I determined that the primary cause of the dissent between Accounting and IT is lack of communication. I am taking my bows! Both Accounting and IT have their own languages, jargon, and buzzwords. Often, each forgets that the other does not speak the same language.

Accounting and IT have a significantly interdependent evolution. Since Mesopotamia, economic growth has fueled the need for accurate information prepared in a timely fashion. Technology advancements throughout history that helped fill this need for fast information include inventions like clay tablets, papyrus, Cuneiform Script, and Arabic numbers. Not all technology advancements involve motherboards and electricity. And of course, not all useful information requires a formal preparation process — "Just the facts, ma'am." Over time we have forgotten that IT and Accounting have a common beginning, like petulant and bickering siblings. Unfortunately, the separate IT and Accounting quests to be the least-hated cost center has caused the departments to become adversarial and many times unprofessional, to the point of detrimental results. Nobody likes IT because the network is slow and you can never get any support. Nobody likes Accounting because they are a big department and don't add any value to the company. IT blames Accounting for the networks being slow because they suck up all the bandwidth, and Accounting blames IT for the large Accounting department because the systems do not work to fully support streamlined financial reporting.

Accounting rule: There are 2 rules for being a successful accountant.
1. **Don't tell them everything you know.**

I noticed that new hires in the IT department are generally put in a position of supporting the Accounting department, such as help-desk or other end-user support roles for accounting applications. I also noticed that they do not stay in this role for long. After speaking with a few of my favorite IT help-desk support staff, I learned that the help-desk staff will get frustrated because the accountants are never happy, regardless of how hard they work to fix the problem. The systems look right, but the accountants still complain. The truth is, the accountants can't effectively communicate what the problems are or why the issues are considered problems.

One of my favorite experiences involved my senior accountant being unable to reconcile the accounts payable balance sheet account. We traced the problem to one invoice; we could see the amount in the vendor ledger and we could see the expense in the general ledger account. The senior accountant entered the help-desk ticket, saying "the accounts payable account will not reconcile. Vendor ledger Company-A shows invoice number #### posted and we find it in the expense." The help-desk response was "…validated the invoice in the vendor ledger and the expense account." Ticket closed. You will learn later in this book that the accounts payable general ledger balance sheet account must be supported by the total of the individual vendor ledgers in the accounts payable module. We will discuss in detail the manual bookkeeping process and how the accounting application has automated it. To preview, an accounting system will create a debit and credit entry to the general ledger and at the same time create an individual ledger card transaction for each vendor and customer. The senior accountant just assumed the help-desk would know this and did not provide any additional detail to the ticket. If the help-desk had just a "little" clue that the ticket did not have the entire issue documented, we could have saved a lot of time. After much frustrating back-and-forth, we finally discovered that the invoice was posted to the accounts payable account using a cost center that should never have been set up. The cost center was not showing up in any of the reports because it was never included in the report design, and the out–of-the-box reports that would have included everything were hidden.

Audit rule: "doveryai no proveryai"[2]
(Trust but verify)

The relationship between Accounting and IT further deteriorated after Sarbanes-Oxley (SOX) was passed in 2002. We will discuss SOX in more detail later in the book. SOX turned every publicly traded company upside down and inside out because of the requirement that the CEO and CFO must attest to the effectiveness of internal controls over financial reporting. Because of the Jobs Act passed by the Obama administration, the Securities and Exchange Commission has been granted unprecedented power to individually prosecute, imprison, and fine members of the board of directors, the CEO, and the CFO for material misstatements identified in the financial statements. These requirements have brought IT processes and procedures under a microscope for both internal and external auditors. Yes, we mean those guys you are extremely fond of and who will probably never go away. The compliance initiatives were extremely expensive and did not appear to create any value. The worst part was the lack of direction from the regulatory agencies, which caused complete chaos for both accounting and IT.

Most IT professionals believe that internal controls are the Accounting department's problem. I began working as an internal auditor for a Fortune 1000 company as part of the SOX compliance implementation. I was performing a walk-through of the sales cycle, which included accounts receivable. A walk-through is a mini in-depth audit that validates, at a high level, the processes in place and where the control points are, and it also assists in proving that management has an understanding of how the process works. The primary objective of this walk-through was to document the process, identifying all of the inputs into the accounting application and determining where the control points are. I learned from the accounts receivable accountant that the sales activity was downloaded from the production system and uploaded into the accounting application by the software engineer. I made my appointment to continue my walk-through with IT. I first asked to see the file and much to my horror, it was a CSV file. We all know that a CSV file can be easily modified using any text editor. I proceeded to ask the software engineer what he did to ensure that the file was not changed between systems and that all the data from the production system was included in the upload to the accounting system. He did not understand why I was asking these questions and his response was "Go away, that is not my problem, I do not have time for this." Hmmm. I was trying to ascertain what the controls were to insure the accuracy and integrity of the data, so the financial statement would be complete and fairly stated. We will discuss what this means later in the book.

Project rule: Good control reveals a problem early, which only means you'll have longer to worry about them.[3]

I was doing some preliminary work to audit a project. The project was to create a global online revenue application. The purpose of this application was to measure customer activity on the company's websites and to give accounting the data necessary to record revenue activity. I was interviewing the project manager and I asked when the audit trail would be developed, so we could tell where the web traffic was coming from. If you do not know, U.S. companies cannot do business with certain countries and individuals on which our government has imposed economic sanctions (we will discuss this later in detail). The response from the project manager was "Phase 8." I said, "Great, what phase is the project at?" He said "Phase 10" – we were behind and over budget and no one cared about the audit trail, so it was eliminated.

Geek rule: Klingon approach to software development: "My software isn't *released*; it escapes, leaving a bloody trail of QA testers in its path!"[4]

We all know that the IT project failure rate is staggering. Some of the primary reasons cited for the failures are lack of project governance, inaccurate business requirements, and poor implementation. All of these reasons lead to one root cause. What could it be? Oh yeah, communication!

I was involved in an implementation of a highly configurable, "off-the-shelf" compliance tracking software program. This implementation was a disaster. During the initial assessment of the various solutions, the senior software engineer vetoed one of the most well-known applications because it was built on outdated technology. The application owner was allowed to override that decision and the purchase was made. The implementation began with a well-thought-out project plan provided by an experienced project manager. As the implementation progressed, we (the end-users) were required to make user interface configuration decisions. At each configuration decision point, I asked what the impact would be on the application performance. The vendor consultant assigned to our account kept saying, "No impact, the software was designed for this." We later found out that the consultant did not really know what the impacts were, because none of their other clients made the same configuration choices. The software engineer who was involved in the product selection (and overruled) didn't want to help; he waved his hands and said "I don't know, it's your system." He was completely frustrated about being overruled, he understood the challenges that the outdated technology would cause, and he did not want to be involved. The project manager didn't know, because her only role was to make sure that the project stayed on schedule. There was no understanding on her part about the application or the user requirements. The bottom line was the hierarchy we designed in the user interface was overly complicated; we were unable to get any workflows to work. Some of the out-of-box reports did not work, because we hid fields that the reports needed, and some of the reports we asked to be created could not be because none of their other clients had asked for them and the system was not designed to handle our requested reporting. Over $80,000 later, we were limping along with the software as best we could. A year and a half after the software went live, the system was abandoned. I realize $80,000 is a small amount of money in comparison to other failed IT projects, but this particular failure highlights several failures: failure to communicate, failure to understand system capabilities, and failure to understand end-user requirements at each level of the project implementation.

I recently followed an online conversation with great interest regarding the level of involvement the chief financial officer (CFO) should have in IT projects. Most of the participants agreed that the CFO should be involved, but the level of participation discussed was limited to the budget, project costs, and the company's strategic plan. While I agree with these points, I believe that there should be greater Accounting department involvement in all IT projects, including the steering committee, the project planning phase and meeting updates; and the quality assurance testing. I don't believe the CFO should be involved at such granular levels, but a knowledgeable accounting professional reporting to the CFO should be.

No matter what the project is, how seemingly insignificant or far removed from the financial statements, I can promise that at some point it will impact the accounting for the company. The obvious impacts are the accounting and reporting for project costs, including recurring maintenance and non-recurring costs. Once the project is live and in production, it may have a direct impact on the financial statements in a number of ways. Did the project result in an asset for the company? Was it properly capitalized? Do we have a reasonable estimate of the useful life so we can depreciate accordingly? If accounting has to use the project for creating entries into the general ledger, do we know that the data is complete and accurate and do we know how to prove it to the auditors? Even a customer relations management (CRM) tool could have impacts that non-accounting personnel would have never considered. What if the CRM was designed to collect information that by law has to be protected, and encryption was never built into the fields requiring protection? That scenario could have significant financial statement impacts, such as disclosing and paying fines and penalties assessed by regulators, paying for credit monitoring for affected customers, and the negative impact to the reputation of the company that may lead financial statement users and other stakeholders to believe that the company will go out of business.

Confucius rule: To know what you know and what you do not know, that is true knowledge.[5]

Why did I write this book? I strongly believe that the information I am presenting will be extremely valuable to the IT professional. During my master's program in IT management at a well-known university, I was required to take an accounting class. By the time the class ended, I realized that my classmates, who were IT professionals, did not learn one thing that would give them enough foundational knowledge to deliver first-class support to the Accounting department. The primary focus of the coursework was recording journal entries to the correct general ledger accounts and generating financial statements, which based on my experience doesn't help troubleshoot issues with the accounting applications. That class was also a wake-up call for me. I realized that there are many layers of BS in accounting that can be attributed to the language that accountants speak.

The intent of this book is to give you a frame of reference and the tools to navigate the BS, not to make you accountants; that's my job and I actually like it. If you hit yourself with a hammer enough times, you will like that as well. The complexity and automation of today's accounting applications make it necessary for any IT or project management professional to be aware of some basic accounting concepts. Communication is the key to solving problems, but we have to ensure that both sides have either a working knowledge of the language or at least an awareness that it exists. Once you completed this book, you will have a basic understanding of "accounting speak," at least to a point where you will know that there is probably more to the story. As you are increasing your ability to communicate with your Accounting department, keep in mind that many accountants will not understand the geek speak associated with information technology and will need your support in translating computer speak.

When working with your Accounting department, keep in mind that many accountants have an inability to communicate in plain terms that are results driven. In short, accountants fail to communicate details and what is needed to measure success. Some accountants have a nasty habit of being too possessive of information that would benefit everyone, even when sharing the information would benefit them as well. Many times, accountants will use accounting rules as big hammers to kill creativity without any real justification; "SOX does not allow that." When you get a help-desk ticket from accounting that seems strange, like the one my senior accountant initiated, there is probably something going on that was not properly communicated. The knowledge you obtain from this book should give you some ideas of the types of questions to ask. If your accountant asks you to implement a control, feel free to ask why. If the accountant answer, "Because SOX requires it," challenge him or her. Ask for details of the risk that is causing concern. If everything else seems reasonable, but the control they want you to perform is not, make alternative suggestions that will achieve the same objective. Every employee in a company is responsible for internal controls. All employees are responsible for communicating problems with operations; compliance issues with the code of conduct, policies, and procedures; and illegal activities, all of which can impact the financial reporting. It is worth repeating, and I will do so several times, that the production of high-quality financial reporting for the company's investor and creditor stakeholders is just as important as delivering high-quality products and services to the company's customers.

If you are facing a long list of projects with very limited resources, use your accountants to help prioritize. A project that decreases expenses by 10% could be far more valuable to the organization than one that increases revenue by 3%. If you are asked to do projects that seem like they will manipulate the books, they probably will. Even if the chief executive officer asked for the project, make sure you understand the intent of the project and what the expected end result is, and then run it by your favorite accountant.

If a project request that collects data from customers is taken through a feasibility study and it is determined that the company will benefit, at least run the proposal by the accountants. Your accountants can help build a project plan that will ensure regulatory and reporting requirements are considered. If security for protected data is required and it is not built into the project plan, then you are immediately increasing your chance of project failure before you even get started. Somewhere during the development process, someone will notice that the data is not protected, causing rework. On the other side of this, never accept a veto from your Accounting department for the simple reason that SOX does not allow it. SOX requires internal controls over financial reporting. If the controls are built into the project, then SOX is not a reason for not moving forward with the project.

Today's enterprise resources planning (ERP) systems are the lifeblood of the global company. The most forgotten fact is that these ERPs grew out of someone's vision to make the accounting function and application more automated. Such as, can we automate the purchasing function and have it interface with the general ledger and accounts payable modules? Can we automate inventory reorder points and inventory usage by integrating inventory management within purchasing and have it interface with the general ledger? Now we have automated production modules, business intelligence, customer resource management, planning, budgeting, and delivery. If you take nothing else from this book, remember that no matter how far removed you believe your IT project to be from the financial statements, because accounting is now a small piece of the ERP, I can promise that at some point the Accounting department will be relying on your project either by using the data as a direct source of reporting or by using data from other systems that directly rely on the new project. I can also promise that when you get those help-desk tickets that are telling you something is wrong, when you can't identify or re-create the issue, there was something missing from the help-desk ticket. With all this in mind, enjoy the book, and I am looking forward to an improved partnership between IT, project management, and accounting.

CHAPTER 1

- FRIGGIN' BEAN COUNTERS -
CAME FROM NOWHERE TO MAKE LIFE MISERABLE

Economic growth is caused by an aggregate increase in demand and/or an aggregate increase in supply or productive capacity. Accounting is a process that takes raw business transactional data and compiles it into useful information for decision makers. Information Technology provides the tools to develop faster methods for compiling raw business transactional data into useful information for decision makers. Since the beginning of civilization, economic growth has influenced the professional practice of accounting, and the accounting profession has been a driving force for bringing information technology to the mainstream.

Many will find the details of this history mind-numbingly boring. A beautifully illustrated and expensive timeline has been prepared to provide the same information without reading the text. If you are so inclined, please enjoy the artwork. This section is important because understanding the history of why anything exists in its current form makes acceptance easier. It is interesting to note that forces occurring in different parts of the world at different times in history have brought us to where we are today. So whether you read the text or review the timeline, please do not blow off this section.

> *In the valley of the Tigris and Euphrates rivers (Mesopotamia) and soon after in the valley of the Nile in Egypt, human beings moved from a life in agricultural villages, using tools of wood, bone, shell, and stone, into a much richer and more varied social organization that we call civilization.*
> ~Donald Kagan, Steven Ozment, & Frank Turner (1987, p. 1)[6]

3150 BC-30 BC: Mesopotamia and Ancient Egypt

Early evidence of accounting records were found in the ruins of the Mesopotamian Valley. These records, dating back more than 7,000 years, indicate that Mesopotamians kept meticulous notes using available technology, such as tally sticks, abacuses, and later, clay tablets. Farmers used accounting methods to track the growth of crops and herds. As the farmers prospered, service-oriented businesses and industries developed. Soon, trading partnerships were developed. Records of what was bought and sold, taxes owed, and trade lists became important records for settling disputes.

The Mesopotamian city-states of Sumeria and Babylon provided unique contributions to the evolution of accounting and information technology. The Sumerians originated the sexagesimal, a base 60 with 12 factors, numeral system during the 3rd millennium BC. To simplify sexagesimal arithmetic, the Sumerian abacus was developed between 2700 and 2300 BC. The Sumerians also developed the earliest known method of writing, cuneiform script. It is recognizable by wedge-shaped indentations on clay tablets using a stylus made of reed. It is believed that a certain character in the cuneiform writing represented the use of the abacus for addition and subtraction. The Babylonians were experts at utilizing available resources to create economic activity. Babylon became a commerce mecca when irrigation methods to control the Euphrates River were perfected. These irrigation methods yielded surplus harvests of grains, vegetables, and fruit, which were supplemented by herds of sheep and cattle. The Babylonians traded food surpluses for raw materials such as copper, gold, and wood, which were used to manufacture weapons, jewelry, and other items that could be traded. Banking firms emerged that devel-

CUNEIFORM SCRIPT

30 BC

CHAPTER 1

oped standard measures for gold and silver and even extended credit.[7]

The first known accountants in the Mesopotamian Valley were called scribes. The scribe would record transactions on clay tablets as described by the parties to the transaction. A wooden rod with a triangular end would be used to record the names of the contracting parties, the goods and money exchanged, and any other promises made.

Egyptian Scribe

The parties signed their names by impressing their unique seals into the clay. The unique seal was an amulet that was worn around the neck of men and included the wearer's name and religion.

Recorded transactions served as memory aids for the farmers and businessmen. Temples, palaces, and private firms employed hundreds of scribes. Scribes were required to write up transactions to ensure that agreements complied with the legal code requirements for commercial transactions. Being a scribe was considered a prestigious profession. The economic growth of these city-states opened additional opportunities for scribes to memorialize transactions.[8]

Egypt became the preeminent civilization in the Mediterranean world. The Egyptians became masters at predicting flooding of the Nile River. Irrigation advances to control the Nile River produced surpluses in crops, creating economic activity, which fueled cultural and social development. The Egyptian economy was controlled by the Pharaoh, who was the absolute ruler.

500 BC — Classical Greece

Ancient Egyptian accountants were known as the eyes and ears of the Pharaoh, keeping detailed records for the network of royal storehouses, which were checked by an elaborate internal verification system. The Egyptians meticulously tracked the movement of commodities; they treated gold and silver as mere articles of exchange without any monetary value.[9]

The books and records of the storehouses were subjected to regular royal audits. These early accountants had good reason to be honest and accurate. If any irregularities were disclosed by royal audits, the accountants were subject to punishment by fine, mutilation, or death.[10]

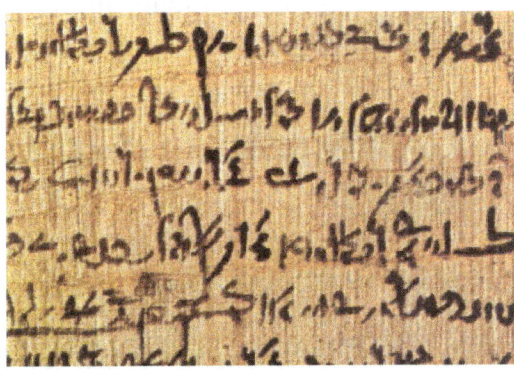
Papyrus

Papyrus eventually replaced clay tablets, providing a more efficient way to produce more detailed records. The papyrus records were important documents, but they confirm that Egyptian accounting never progressed beyond simple list making in its thousands of years of existence.

Classical Greek Coin

500 BC - 401 BC: Classical Greece

The invention of money was the most significant contribution to accountancy and economic growth made by Classical Greece in the 5th century BC[11]. Local money was the only currency Classical Greek merchants would take in exchange for goods and services. Public accountants were used by the

CHAPTER 1 15

citizens to maintain real authority and control over government finances. Members of the Athens popular Assembly legislated financial matters and controlled the receipt and expenditure of public monies through the oversight of 10 state accountants[12].

By influencing Roman culture, Classical Greece is provided the foundation for modern Western culture.

27 BC - 14 AD: Ancient Rome

As the use of money as a means of exchange for goods and services gained acceptance, formalized accounting began to take shape in ancient Rome. When governments began levying taxes, the need for household record-keeping evolved. Daily entries of receipts and payments were kept in a day book by the head of the family. Monthly postings were made to a cashbook known as a codex accepti et expensi. Tracking household expenses became necessary because citizens were required to submit regular statements of assets and liabilities to the government.[13] The government used these statements as the basis for determining citizenship and assessing taxes.

RomanCoin

27 BC — Ancient Rome

The most significant Roman contribution to accounting was the use of annual budgets. The budgets attempted to coordinate the Empire's diverse financial enterprises; limit expenditures to the amount of estimated revenues, and levy taxes in a manner which took into consideration the citizen's ability to pay. Roman accountants, called quaestors, developed and maintained elaborate systems of checks and balances for governmental receipts and disbursements. Quaestors were elite members of society that reported directly to the emperor. Public accounts were examined by an audit staff. The quaestors were required to account to their successors and the Roman senate upon leaving office.[14]

15 BC - 1300 AD: Medieval Accounting

The medieval period or the middle ages of European history laid the foundation for two of today's most important accounting concepts. Stewardship is an ethical principal that embodies the responsible planning and management of resources. Conservatism is known today as the doctrine of prudence in accounting. However, the medieval period is considered a period of stagnation in the evolution of both accounting and information technology.

William the Conqueror

In 1086 BC, William the Conqueror conducted a survey (known as the Doomsday Book) of all real estate that he took possession of in the name of the king, as a means to collect taxes due. The oldest surviving accounting record in the English language is the Pipe Roll or the "Great Roll of the Exchequer,"[15] which gave an annual description of rents, fines, and taxes due to the King of England from 1130 AD - 1830 AD.

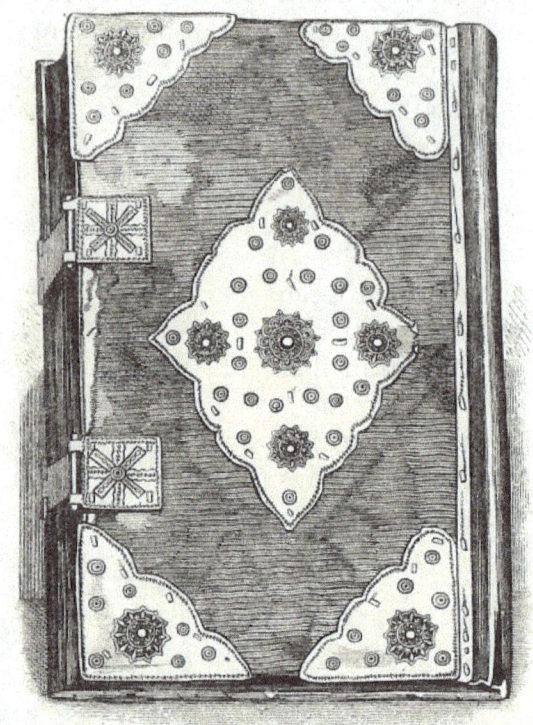

During the medieval era, tax collection was performed by the sheriff and accounting functions were performed by a treasurer. Once the sheriff collected the taxes due, the treasurer would cut a notch in a tally stick as a record of the transaction.

BINDING OF THE DOOMSDAY BOOK

15 BC — *Medieval Accounting*

18 FRIGGIN' BEAN COUNTERS

1301 AD - 1600 AD: Italian Renaissance

The Italians of the Renaissance are acknowledged as the fathers of modern accounting. They elevated trade and commerce to new levels, resulting in a need for methods to determine profits. The Renaissance is the first time Arabic numerals (0, 1, 2, 3, 4, 5, 6, 7, 8, and 9) were used to track business accounts. Extensive business records were kept because the use of economic capital and credit grew to a larger scale.

The double-entry method of bookkeeping was introduced during the Italian Renaissance. Double-entry bookkeeping is where each transaction, or event, entered into the accounting records has at least two offsetting entries. While the conceptual origins of double-entry bookkeeping are subject to debate, the earliest evidence of a prototype double-entry system can be traced to a Florentine merchant, named Amatino Manucci, from the later 13th century. The oldest records of a complete double-entry bookkeeping system are from

CA 1459 GERMAN MANUSCRIPT TEACHING ARABIC NUMERALS

CHAPTER 1 19

the Republic of Genoa in 1340. These records included accounts that contain debits and credits journalized in such a way that two or more accounts were affected. Account balances were carried forward from the previous year. By the end of the 15th century, this system of bookkeeping became widely used by bankers and merchants.

Accounting and information technology have evolved together, each influencing the other and both acting in response to economic growth. Technology advancements are more than motherboards and transistors. For the time periods discussed in this chapter, clay tablets, cuneiform script, coins, and paper were high-tech conveniences. Since the beginning of civilization, economic activity has created a need for information. The need for information has caused accountants to leverage available technology advances to provide the needed information.

1301 AD *Italian Renaissance*

Three accountants and three engineers are travelling by train to a conference. Each accountant buys a ticket while the three engineers buy a single ticket. One accountant asks, "How are three people going to travel on one ticket?" "Watch and see," replies an engineer. They board the train; the accountants take their seats, while the three engineers cram into the restroom and close the door.

Shortly after the train departs, the conductor comes by collecting tickets. He knocks on the restroom door and says, "Tickets please." A single arm emerges from a crack in the door. The conductor takes the ticket and moves on. The accountants were impressed and agreed it was a great idea.

On the trip back, the accountants buy one ticket, but the engineers don't buy any. Perplexed, one accountant asks, "How are you going to travel without a ticket?" "Watch and see," answers an engineer.

When they board the train, the three accountants cram into one restroom and the three engineers cram into another. When the train departs, one of the engineers knocks on the restroom the accountants are in and says, "Tickets please."[141]

1600 AD

CHAPTER 2

– FRIGGIN' BEAN COUNTERS – STOLE OUR COMPUTERS

On two occasions I have been asked, 'Pray, Mr. Babbage, if you put into the machine wrong figures, will the right answers come out?' I am not able rightly to apprehend the kind of confusion of ideas that could provoke such a question.

~CHARLES BABBAGE (1864, P. 67)

BLAISE PASCAL

Now that we have established that accounting and information technology grew up together, we shall see how the growth in information technology commenced the Industrial Revolution, causing explosive economic growth, which drove a need for faster, more accurate, and precise financial reporting.

1601 AD - 1700 AD: Europe's Early Modern Period

The 17th century marks the early modern period in Europe. This period included many historically significant events in the evolution of economic activity, accounting, and most significantly, information technology.

Blaise Pascal[17] (1623 –1662), a French mathematician, physicist, inventor, and Christian philosopher, invented the first mechanical calculating machine. The mechanical calculating machine was conceived as a way to help his father, a tax

PASCALINE CALCULATOR (PASCAL 1642)

collector.[18] Work began in 1642, with the first working prototype ready in 1645. Unfortunately, the mechanical calculating machine was a commercial failure because it was expensive to produce. Over the next decade, Pascal built 20 machines, making improvements to each one. The primary machine operation was to add and subtract directly and to multiply and divide by repetition. Pascal's work started the evolution of the adding machine and is considered an early forerunner to computer engineering. To honor Pascal for his contributions, the Pascal programming language was introduced in 1970. Pascal programming is structured and is a component of the original Macintosh operating system.

Gottfried Wilhelm Von Leibniz[19] (1646 – 1716) was a German mathematician and philosopher. He worked to improve Pascal's mechanical calculating machine by adding automatic multiplication and division. His work resulted in the development of the Leibniz wheel in 1673. The Leibniz wheel is a cylinder with a set of teeth of incremental lengths that is coupled to a counting wheel. The Leibniz wheel was used in mechanical calculators for the next three centuries, until the invention of the electronic calculator in the mid-1960s.

LEIBNIZ WHEEL

1700 AD

1801 AD – 1900 AD: The 19th Century and the Industrial Revolutions

The first Industrial Revolution began around 1760 in England and quickly spread to the rest of the world. This period is noted for the transition to new manufacturing processes, which influenced every aspect of daily life until 1840. The second Industrial Revolution soon began and continued until 1870, a transitional period when technology and economic activity gained momentum. Steam-powered engines and factories led to large scale manufacturing. This was also the period when accounting began looking like a cohesive profession with standards of practice, ethical behaviors, and professional designations.

Birth of the Accounting Profession

Scotland is the birthplace of the accounting profession as we know it today. The practice of accounting was closely associated with the profession of law. There are several instances where members of the Society of Writers to Her Majesty's Signet practiced as accountants. Writers to the Signet had the special privilege of drawing up documents required to be signeted (signed or marked with a specific seal). Today, the Society is an independent, non-regulatory association of solicitors (lawyers).

The Glasgow, Scotland, Institute of Accountants petitioned Queen Victoria for a grant of a Royal Charter July 6, 1854. The Petition was signed by 49 institute members and set forth:

…that the profession of an accountant has long existed in Scotland as a distinct profession

ARITHMOMETER

of great respectability; originally the number of practicing accountants was few but the number has been rapidly increasing, and the profession in Glasgow now embraces a numerous as well as highly respectable body of persons. The business of an accountant requires, for the proper prosecution of it, considerable and varied attainments; that it is not confined to the department of the Actuary, which forms indeed only a branch of it, but that, while it comprehends all matters connected with arithmetical calculation, or involving investigation into figures, it also ranges over a much wider field, in which a considerable acquaintance with the general principles of law, and a knowledge in particular of the Law of Scotland, is quite indispensable.

That accountants are frequently employed by Courts of Law to aid those Courts in their investigation of matters of Accounting, which involve, to a greater or less extent, points of law of more or less difficulty; that they act under such remits very much as the Masters in Chancery are understood to act in England, and that it is obvious that to the due performance of a profession such as this a liberal education is essential. Directly after its formation the Edinburgh Society deliberated upon a distinctive title for its members and resolved to adopt the name of 'Chartered Accountant', indicated by the letters C.A.[20]

CHARLES XAVIER THOMAS DE COLMAR

Visionaries Begin the Computer Evolution!

ANALYTICAL ENGINE

Charles Xavier Thomas de Colmar[21] (1785 – 1870) was a French inventor and entrepreneur. He is known for designing, patenting, and manufacturing the first commercially successful mechanical calculator. The Leibniz wheel made the design and reliability of the Arithmometer possible. The Arithmometer was introduced in 1820 and became commercially available in 1852, proving to be reliable and dependable enough to be used in an office environment. It was manufactured until 1914. The Arithmometer launched the mechanical calculator industry and led to the development of the electronic calculator and the first commercially available personal computer in the 1970s.

Charles Babbage[22] (1791–1871) was an English mathematician, philosopher, inventor, and mechanical engineer. He contributed to the mechanical calculator industry by inventing the Differential Engine. The Differential Engine was designed to calculate polynomial functions, which are used in cost accounting. While working on the Differential Engine, Babbage realized that a more general design was possible. He conceptually invented the first mechanical programmable computer, called the Analytical Engine. The Analytical Engine design incorporated arithmetic logic, conditional branching and loops, and integrated memory. Unfortunately, the Analytical Engine would not be built in Babbage's lifetime due to conflicts with staff and inadequate funding.

CHARLES BABBAGE

Augusta Ada King, Countess of Lovelace[23] (1815 – 1852), was an English mathematician, the only daughter of poet/author Lord Byron, and is considered the first computer programmer.

PUNCH CARD

AUGUSTA ADA KING

28 FRIGGIN' BEAN COUNTERS

The Countess and Charles Babbage were friends. She supplemented his work on the Differential Engine with her "Notes" in 1843. The Notes included what is recognized as the first algorithm intended to be processed by the Analytical Engine. The Countess of Lovelace's visionary speculation asserted that the Analytical Engine would act upon other things beside numbers. Symbols could be manipulated according to a defined set of rules and numbers could represent entities. The Notes marked the transition from calculation to computation.

Herman Hollerith

Herman Hollerith[24] (1860 –1929) was an American statistician and inventor. Under contract with the U.S. Census Bureau, he developed a punch card mechanical tabulator that compiled the 1890 census data in one year. The data from the 1880 census took 8 years to compile into usable statistics. The tabulating machine was an electromechanical machine that assisted in summarizing information using punch cards as the primary medium for input of both computer programs and data. Hollerith founded the Tabulating Machine Company that later merged to become International Business Machines (IBM). Hollerith is regarded as the father of modern automatic computation. Tabulating machines were embraced by organizations. In 1903, Marshall Field began using the tabulating machine for department store sales analysis. In 1904, the Pennsylvania Steel Company implemented the use of the tabulating machine for cost accounting, primarily using labor and machine hours as inputs. After 1904, commercial use of the tabulating machine steadily increased.[25]

Tabulating Machine

By the middle of the 19th century, England was enjoying prosperous times brought on by the Industrial Revolution. The demand for qualified accountants increased with financial prosperity. In 1880, the Institute of Chartered Accountants in England and Wales brought together all accountancy organizations in those countries. The membership started with 587 members, and an additional 606 were enrolled based on their experience. The Institute established the first standards of conduct, admission examinations, and professional designations, the Fellow Chartered Accountant (FCA) and the Associate Chartered Accountant (ACA).[26]

The Accounting Profession Moves to the United States!

During this same period, England was making large capital investments in the United States. Scottish and British accountants traveled to the U.S. to audit these investments, and many stayed to set up practice. By 1886, there were more than 200 accounting firms. In 1887, these firms joined to form the American Association of Public Accountants, which officially became the American Institute of Certified Public Accountants (AICPA) in 1957.[27]

The founding of the AICPA established accountancy as a profession in the U.S. Today, the AICPA represents over 660,000 Certified Public Accountants (CPAs) in the United States.

The AICPA acts as an advocate before legislative bodies, public interest groups, and other professional organizations. The AICPA develops standards for auditing of private companies and other services performed by CPAs. Additionally, the AICPA provides educational opportunities and monitors and enforces compliance with the profession's technical and ethical standards.[28]

The law establishing the CPA designation was passed in New York on April 17, 1896.[29]

The National Uniform CPA Exam is set by the AICPA and administered by the National Association of State Boards of Accountancy (NASBA). The AICPA was the premier rule-making and standards-setting body that oversaw the accounting profession. Until the failure of Enron and the downfall of Arthur Andersen, the AICPA was the governing

1901 AD — *20th Century and Automation*

rule-setting body for the professional practice of accounting.[30]

It is important to understand that while all CPAs are accountants, not all accountants are CPAs. The CPA designation is distinguished by rigorous educational requirements, high professional standards, a strict code of professional ethics, a state licensing status, and a strong commitment to serving the public interest.

The CPA in public practice is required to maintain an active state license because they are generating financial statements or performing audits that are relied on by the public at large. Today, CPAs in public practice bear a significant amount of professional and personal liability for the quality of their work.

An active license status requires the CPA to meet a set number of professional educational requirements, usually every two years, and to pass a test on ethical practices. This ensures that the CPA is current on new developments in the accounting profession and other regulatory agencies that may impact the way a CPA performs their work.

CPAs working for companies can have an active or inactive license; however, in most states, a CPA with an inactive license must disclose that fact. A CPA with an inactive license is generally not required to meet the same rigorous continuing educational requirements that an active licensee has to meet. This is the primary reason a CPA will allow his or her license to become inactive.

From the invention of the abacus to the late 1800s, accounting was a manual process. Transactions imprinted in clay tablets evolved into entries handwritten into journals and ledgers. Although the available technologies were manual in nature, they provided efficiency and accuracy in the accounting. The development of information technologies was the result of visionary mathematicians, engineers, and inventors looking

to solve information-gathering problems effectively and accurately. The demand for the accounting profession to provide better, more accurate, and faster information for management decision-making has been instrumental in bringing new information technologies to the mainstream. As automated technologies become widely used, the need to set standards for consistent and comparable financial reporting quickly became apparent.

1901 – 1939: The Computer Evolution Begins!

Vannevar Bush

Differential Analyzer at NASA

Vannevar Bush[31] (1890–1974) was an American engineer, inventor, science administrator, and professor at the Massachusetts Institute of Technology (MIT). Beginning in 1927, Bush supervised the construction of the Differential Analyzer with MIT students. The Differential Analyzer is an analog computer that solves differential equations with as many as 18 independent variables. The Differential Analyzer had both electrical and mechanical components. It could store numbers used for counting or quantities from measurement. The work earned Bush the title of "Father of the Electronic Computer."

Claude Elwood Shannon[32] (1916 – 2001) was an American mathematician, electronic engineer, and cryptographer known as "the Father of Information Theory." Shannon's work with Bush at MIT

1940 AD — Second Generation Computers

was the beginning of digital circuit design theory. Working on the analytical engine, Shannon described the application of Boolean algebra to electronic circuits in his landmark master's thesis. Shannon also published a paper in the 1950's titled "Programming a Computer for Playing Chess," describing how a computer could play a reasonable game.

Howard Hathaway Aiken[33] (1900 – 1973) was an American electrical engineer, physicist, inventor, and computer programmer. Inspired by Charles Babbage's work, he built the Automatic Sequence Controlled Calculator (ASCC) computer from 1940 to 1943 while working as a professor at Harvard University. The project was funded by IBM and used rolls of punched paper rather than cards to program the computer. The ASCC, later renamed the Harvard Mark I,[34] was the first machine that could execute long computations automatically. The computer was a massive machine with a steel frame 51 feet long and eight feet high. The calculator consisted of an interlocking panel of small gears, counters, switches, and control circuits. The ASCC used 500 miles of wire with three million connections, 3,500 multipole relays with 35,000 contacts, 2,225 counters, 1,464 tenpole switches, and tiers of 72 adding machines.[35] It was the largest electromechanical calculator built to date.

HOWARD AIKEN

ASCC – I/O DEVICES

1940 – 1956: First Generation Computers

1956 AD

CHAPTER 2 33

ENIAC

First generation computers are identified as the most expensive to build and operate, with enormous devices that used vacuum tubes for circuits and magnetic drums for memory. Basically, first generation computers were little more than calculators that cost up to $4,250,000 in today's dollars.

Vacuum Tubes

Dr. J. Presper Eckert (1919 – 1995), an American electrical engineer, and Dr. John Mauchly (1907 –1980), an American physicist, partnered to build the Electronic Numeric Integrator and Calculator (ENIAC) in 1942 while working at the Moore School of Electrical Engineering at the University of Pennsylvania.[36] The ENIAC cost $500,000 to build and was financed by the United States Army. The project was announced to the world in 1946 and was heralded as the Giant Brain. The ENIAC introduced vacuum technology, eliminating the need for mechanical parts and increasing the speed of calculations. The computer weighed 27 tons and took up 1,800 square feet.

Eckert and Mauchly next built the Electronic Discrete Variable Automatic Computer (EDVAC). The EDVAC was one of the earliest electronic binary serial computers, with automatic addition, subtraction, multiplication, programmed division, and automatic checking.[37]

Eckert (standing) & Mauchly

1964 AD — Second Generation Computers — 1971 AD

Dr. Eckert and Dr. Mauchly formed the Eckert-Mauchly Computer Corporation (EMCC) in 1946 to build computers for commercial use. EMCC was acquired by Remington-Rand Corporation, which became the Sperry-Rand Corporation and is now known as Unisys.[38]

Early Integrated Circuit by RCA

The UNIVersal Automated Computer (UNIVAC) was the second commercial computer, built in the U.S. by Eckert and Mauchly. The UNIVAC was the first computer to be used in business and was designed for the fast execution of large amounts of simple arithmetic calculations and data transport operations.[39] The U.S. Census Bureau was the first to purchase UNIVAC on March 31, 1951.[40] Other early adopters of the UNIVAC technology include the U.S. Air Force, the U.S. Army Map Service, the AC Nielsen Company, and the Prudential Insurance Company.

Sir Maurice Vincent Wilkes

Sir Maurice Vincent Wilkes[41] (1913 – 2010) was a British computer scientist. He and his team at Cambridge University built the Electronic Delay Storage Automatic Computer (EDSAC). The design was based on a 1945 publication titled "First Draft of a Report on the EDVAC," by John Von Neumann, an American mathematician. The report described the logical design of a computer using stored programs. The EDSAC successfully stored programs, with the first program successfully executed in May 1949. The program calculated a table of squares and a list of prime numbers.

Third Generation Computers

NOW AD

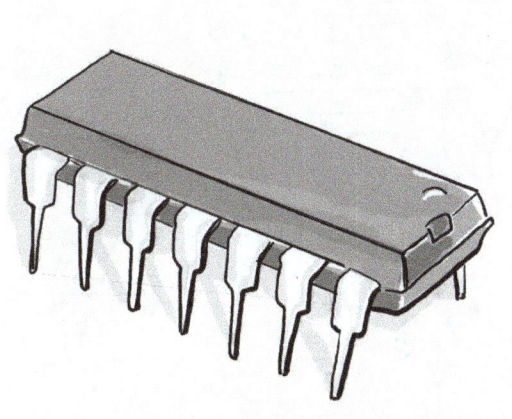

CHAPTER 2 **35**

1956 – 1963: Second Generation Computers

The second generation of computers used transistors rather than vacuum tube technology. The first patent for the transistor principle was filed in Canada by Austrian-Hungarian physicist Julius Edgar Lilienfeld on October 22, 1925. A subsequent patent was filed in 1934 by German physicist Dr. Oskar Heil.

WILLIAM SHOCKLEY

William Bradford Shockley (1910 –1989) was an American physicist and inventor. Shockley and his team, composed of Walter Brattain and John Bardeen, built the first working transistor for Bell Labs in 1947. The introduction of transistors into computer technology allowed computers to become smaller and faster, less expensive to build and operate, and more reliable.[42]

Additional contributions to the 2nd generation of computers are as follows:

- Bell Laboratories completed the TRADIC in January 1954.
- IBM announced the IBM 608 transistor calculator in April 1955, the first commercially sold, all solid-state computing machine.
- The Philco Transac S-1000 scientific computer and the S-2000 electronic data processing computer were the first commercially produced transistor computers, introduced in 1957.

36 FRIGGIN' BEAN COUNTERS

1964 – 1971: Third Generation Computers

The integrated circuit marked the start of the third generation of computers. The integrated circuit is composed of interconnected transistors, resistors, and capacitors constructed on one semiconductor to perform a defined function. Integrated circuits allowed for the continued evolution of computers. The first patent was issued in 1949, to Werner Jacobi, of Siemens AG, for an integrated-circuit-like semiconductor amplifying device.[43]

Geoffrey Dummer

Geoffrey W. A. Dummer[44] (1909 – 2002), a radar scientist working for the British Ministry of Defense, introduced the idea of the integrated circuit at a symposium in Washington DC in May 1952. Unfortunately, Dummer could not successfully build a working integrated circuit.

Jack St. Clair Kilby (1923 –2005) was an American electrical engineer who demonstrated the first working integrated circuit in September 1958, while working for Texas Instruments.[45]

Kilby partnered with Robert Norton Noyce (1927 – 1990) to co-found the Fairchild Semiconductor in 1957 and the Intel Corporation in 1968. Noyce and Kilby are credited with the invention of the integrated circuit, or microchip, which fueled the personal computer revolution and gave Silicon Valley its name. Noyce was nicknamed "the Mayor of Silicon Valley."[46]

Robert Noyce

The integrated circuit began appearing in computers in 1963. Third generation

CHAPTER 2 37

computers were designed for general purpose computing. They were the first machines that users interacted with using monitors, keyboards, operating systems, and applications.

INTEGRATED CIRCUIT

1971 – NOW: Fourth Generation Computers

Microprocessors are thousands of integrated circuits built into one chip, which became known as Large Scale Integration technology. The Intel 4004 microprocessor was developed in 1971.[48]

ADVERTISEMENT FOR THE 8080

The first microcomputers were introduced in the early '70s as kits and then as pre-built machines in the mid '70s for hobbyists and developers. They were primarily teaching tools for the use of microprocessors. Early microcomputers were rarely used with pre-written application software, as pre-written software was rare and expensive.

The Intel 8080-MOS 6502 processors became available in 1978 and drastically reduced the cost of computer hardware. The first microcomputer for the home user was sold by IBM in 1981. Apple soon followed in 1984 with the Macintosh. As these computers became more powerful, they could be linked together to form networks. This networking capability lead to the development of the Internet and, most recently, cloud computing.[49]

NOW and Beyond: Fifth Generation Computers

Fifth generation computers are currently being developed around artificial intelligence. This technology includes the voice recognition capabilities in use today. The history for this section is being written as we live our lives.

How is the Evolution of Computers Related to Accounting?

In the early years, the central focus of the development of computer technology was hardware. First-, second-, and third-generation computers needed programmers to write the instructions that machines needed to perform tasks. UNIVAC and ENIAC relied on machine language for executable instructions but could solve only one problem at a time. Machine language is the lowest level of programming language and consists of a set of symbolic

1984 MACINTOSH BY APPLE

instruction codes, usually in binary form (1's and 0's). The inputs were punch cards or paper tape and the outputs were paper printouts.

The second generation of computers used assembly language, which turned to focus to software development. Assembly language allowed programmers to write computer instructions in words. High-level programming languages, such as COBOL and FORTRAN, were in development at that time. The adoption and use of computers by businesses and then by the home user spawned the growth of the packaged software industry. Accounting applications emerged to the meet record-keeping needs of individuals and businesses. Today, accounting applications and enterprise resource planning (ERP) systems have grown into a multibillion dollar global industry. Some key examples are provided below.

SAP AG is a European multinational software corporation that makes enterprise software capable of managing business operations and customer relations. SAP is headquartered in Germany and has regional offices around the world. The initial release of its first financial accounting system, known as SAP R/1, occurred in 1973. The application permitted the use of centralized data storage and improved data maintenance by offering a common system for multiple tasks. The system ran on IBM servers and used the DOS operating system.[50]

Peachtree accounting software was developed in an Atlanta computer store and released in 1976. Peachtree was the first commercial software available to consumers for their accounting needs. In 1981, Peachtree was bundled with the first IBM PC shipped to home users.[51]

VisiCalc was the first commercially available spreadsheet package and was originally released with the Apple II in 1980. VisiCalc was developed to simplify complex, time-consuming financial analysis. VisiCalc is credited with turning the microcomputer from a hobby for computer enthusiasts into a serious business tool.[52]

Intuit was founded in 1993 by Scott Cook and Tom Prolix. Cook's work at Proctor & Gamble helped him realize that personal computers would become the replacement for manual accounting systems. The first version of Quicken was released in 1984. Prolix coded Quicken in Microsoft's BASIC programming language for the IBM PC and in UCSD Pascal for the Apple II. The software was designed to look like a checkbook and quickly gained wide popularity.[53]

From the abacus to the calculator to the computer, throughout history, economic growth has created a need for accounting and accountants to provide information that is accurate and relevant. The information must be timely to be useful and meaningful to decision makers. Accounting as a profession has existed since the dawn of civilization. The evolution of information technology and the development of accounting software packages have been instrumental in the evolution of the global economy.

> *The Accounting profession is as old as the oldest profession. Some might ask, "What is the difference between a prostitute and an accountant? One charges by the hour, creates outrageous fantasies for clients and can't tell people what they do for a living. The other is a prostitute.*[54]

CHAPTER 3

– FRIGGIN' BEAN COUNTERS –
KEEP YOUR RULES

*You have to learn the rules of the game.
And then you have to play better than anyone else.*

~Albert Einstein[55]

There are a significant number of accounting rules that must be followed, such as when and how to recognize and record revenue or when a public company must make financial statements available to the public. There are numerous rule-setting bodies in the U.S. and internationally. In many cases, accounting rules are seemingly unreasonable. Information technology projects that do not conform to, do not support, or somehow violate these rules will experience cost overruns, reworks, and probably failure. These rules have evolved over the millennia that accounting has existed and are generally born out of the need for more comparable financial data among companies in the same industries, regulatory requirements, fraudulent behaviors, and accounting scandals.

Old Rules Never Change: They Just Get More Restrictive

The oldest example of written laws and rules affecting accounting can be found in Babylon. The Code of Hammurabi dates back to 1772 BC. The Code enacted 282 laws and outlines the associated punishment for breaking those laws. The Code set contract law and provides guidance on commercial transactions and payments, such as wages to be paid, terms of transactions, and builder liabilities. It also set standardized weights and measures and defined family and household relationships like divorce, paternity, and sexual behavior.[57]

Code of Hammurabi

Court records discovered in Egypt document that the laws there were based on the Pharaoh's common-sense view of right and wrong; however, no documented legal codes survived the ages. Surviving records provide evidence that members of Egyptian society were encouraged to reach agreements and resolve conflicts without court intervention.[58]

Augustus of Prima Porta

The Deeds of the Divine Augustus are a record of the Roman Emperor Augustus' liberal and generous spirit. Emperor Augustus, founder of the Roman Empire, ruled from 27 BC until his death in 14 AD. The records quantify government distributions to the citizens such as grants of land or money to army veterans, subsidies to the treasury, the building of temples, religious offerings, and spending

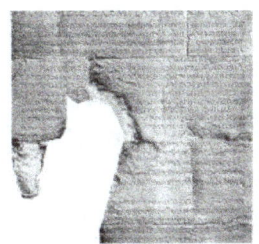
THE DEEDS

for theatrical shows and gladiatorial games. The accounting significance of The Deeds is that they represent a detailed record of financial information covering a forty-year period. The records remained accessible to government officials, and there are indications that these records were used for planning and decision making.

The first set of formalized accounting rules was published in 1494 by Luca Pacioli during the Italian Renaissance. The work, written as a digest and guide to existing mathematical knowledge, was titled *Summa de Arithmetic, Geometria, Proportioni et Proportionalita,* which translates to Everything About Arithmetic, Geometry and Proportion. Bookkeeping was one of five topics covered in the chapter titled "De Computis et Scripturas" ("Of Reckonings and Writings").

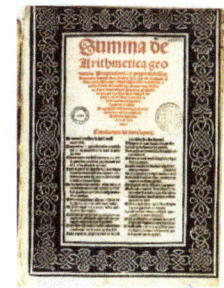
COVER OF SUMMA DE ARITHMETIC

PORTRAIT OF PACIOLI

The chapter provides detailed commerce instruction to the Duke of Urbano for conducting business and to traders needing immediate information about their assets and liabilities:[59]

To be successful, the merchant needs three things:

1) sufficient cash or credit;
2) good bookkeepers; and
3) an accounting system which allows him to view his finances at a glance (1494).[60]

Before commencing business, the merchant should prepare an inventory of all business and personal assets and debts. The inventory must be completed in one day, with any property appraised at the current market values. The inventory should then be arranged according to mobility and value, with cash and other valuables listed first, since they are most easily lost (2002, p. 9).[61]

Additional chapters of the work describe the fundamental system of books and accounts. All business transactions are to be recorded in a journal in chronological order, in the monetary units used, and later converted to a common currency for double-entry ledger posting. Double-entry posting requires a debit and an equal credit. While the origin of the terms debit and credit are unknown, it is believed that the terms evolved from the *Summa*. The Latin words debere (to owe) and credere (to entrust) were used to describe the two sides of a double-entry transaction. The journal is the merchant's private account book. Entries consisted of a narrative debit, credit, and explanation in one continuous paragraph.[62] A ledger is where the bookkeeper posts all transactions, such as sales and purchasing transactions; cash in hand is posted as a debit, just as it was entered in the journal.

The trial balance is the end of Paoli's bookkeeping cycle. Debit amounts for the ledger are listed on the left side of the balance sheet and credits are listed on the right. If the two are equal, the ledger is in balance.[63]

The double-entry bookkeeping method is still used today and is the basic principle behind all of the commercially available accounting applications. The primary differences between today's accounting and the methods described by Paoli are the refinements brought about because of larger-scale business operations and technology advancements.

Wait, Didn't You Say the AICPA Was the Accounting Oversight?

It is an indisputable fact that rules and laws are created when things go wrong. The larger the wrong is, the more pervasive the laws and rules are. Laws are intended to prevent harm to others. White collar crime is a nonviolent crime that is committed for financial gain. Crimes that are committed for financial gain generally involve manipulating financial results because assets have been misappropriated or liabilities and expenses are not recorded or too much income is recorded. Asset misappropriation is an all-encompassing phrase that includes stealing cash and property. White collar crimes are committed by greedy individuals who are acting in their own self-interest, but technology must also share some of the responsibility. The same advancements that have made information available faster also made the information easier to manipulate and created gateways for more sophisticated ways to misappropriate assets.

Other than the double-entry bookkeeping rules, there were no standard accounting frameworks for U.S. companies prior to the 1930s. New accounting rules are created as a reaction to evolving transactions, the needs of financial statement users, or corporate scandals. In the early years, the rules began to evolve, but adherence to and enforcement of the rules remained questionable.

The first major accounting scandal that came to public attention was a case called Ultramares Corporation v. Touche in 1934. Every accounting student studies this case because it was the first case that established auditor liability. The Ultramares Corp. of London loaned a significant amount of money to Fred Stern & Company, a New York importer. The accounts receivable was used to secure that loan and the decision by Ultramares to move forward was based on the strength of the 1924 audited financial statement. Fred Sterns & Company filed for bankruptcy in 1925. Touche, Niven & Co., the predecessor to Deloitte and Touche, had given the company a clean audit opinion, after failing to discover that management was overstating the accounts receivable. The auditors knew that the accounts receivable would be used to secure the loan, so the courts ruled that the auditor had been negligent because of the failure to discover the insolvency of Fred Stern & Company. This case coincided with the stock market crash that led to the Great Depression. The government needed to restore public trust since the number of users of accounting information was growing.

Other notable cases that led to new rules and requirements are:

- 1937 - Interstate Hosiery Mills, a company that had an exclusive unlimited license to produce a patented pointed toe stocking, became involved in a fraudulent stock manipulation case. The company's independent accountant, Raymond Marieh, employed with Homes and Davis, inflated the value of the company's assets by 40% of book value, creating 1.9 million dollars of fictitious assets. This case led to the establishment of the first accounting standards. Accounting standards are a set of rules designed to make financial statements comparable across similar industries.

- 1938 - McKesson & Robbins, now the pharmaceutical company McKesson Corporation, was caught generating bogus sales documents. The company had been taken over by Phillip Musica, a convicted felon. He used fake names to take control of both McKesson & Robbins and Adelphia Pharmaceutical. Musica employed family members to generate the bogus sales documents to pay commissions to a shell distribution company under his control. The company treasurer, Julian Thompson, discovered the fraud. At that time, it was also discovered that $20 million of the $87 million in assets on the balance sheet were phony. This case resulted in the requirement that every public company have an audit committee.

- 2001 - Enron Corporation, an American energy company based in Houston, TX, filed for bankruptcy protection when it was discovered that the reported financial condition was a creatively planned accounting fraud. Enron's audit firm, Arthur Andersen, was accused of applying reckless auditing standards. This case resulted in the passage of the Sarbanes-Oxley Act (SOX) and the creation of the Public Company Accounting Oversight Board (PCAOB); both of these topics will be discussed later in detail.

Unfortunately, accounting scandals have been the driving force behind the creation of many new accounting rules and ultimately the creation of the PCAOB and passing of the SOX legislation. The AICPA was the accounting profession oversight board and responsible for self-regulation by peer review. Up until the Enron scandal, the accounting profession was the only self-regulating profession in the U.S.

Who Makes the Rules?

	U.S. GAAP - Codification of Accounting Standards
105	GAAP Hierarchy
105	GAAP History
205	Presentation of Financial Statements
205-20	Discontinued Operations
210	Balance Sheet
210-20	Offsetting
220	Comprehensive Income
225	Income Statement
225-20	Extraordinary and Unusual Items
230	Statement of Cash Flows
250	Accounting Changes and Error Corrections
260	Earnings per Share
270	Interim Reporting
310	Impairment of a Loan
320	Investment Securities
320	Other-Than-Temporary Impairments, FSP FAS 115-2
320-10-05	Overview of Investments in Other Entities
320-10-35	Reclassification of Investments in Securities
323-10	Equity Method Investments
323-30	Investments in Partnerships and Joint Ventures
325-20	Cost Method Investments
330	Inventory
340-20	Capitalized Advertising Costs
350-20	Goodwill
350-30	Intangibles Other than Goodwill
350-40	Internal-Use Software
350-50	Website Development Costs
360	Property, Plant and Equipment
360-20	Real Estate Sales
410	Asset Retirement and Environmental Obligations
420	Exit or Disposal Cost Obligations
450	Contingencies
450-20	Loss Contingencies
450-30	Gain Contingencies
480	Redeemable Financial Instruments
505-20	Stock Dividends, Stock Splits
505-30	Treasury Stock
605	SEC Staff Accounting Bulletin, Topic 13
605-25	Revenue Recognition - Multiple Element Arrangements
805	Business Combinations
810	Consolidation
810	Noncontrolling Interests
810	Consolidation of Variable Interest Entities, SFAS 167
815	Derivatives and Hedging Overview
820	Fair Value Measurements
820	Fair value when the markets are not active, FSP FAS 157-4
825	Fair Value Option
830	Foreign Currency Matters
830-20	Foreign Currency Transactions
830-30	Translation of Financial Statements
835	Interest
835-20	Capitalization of Interest
835-30	Imputation of Interest
840	Leases
840-20	Operating Leases
840-30	Capital Leases
840-40	Sale-Leaseback Transactions
845	Nonmonetary Transactions
855	Subsequent Events
860-20	Sale of Financial Assets, SFAS 166
860-50	Servicing Assets and Liabilities, SFAS 156
985-20	Costs of software to be sold

HTTP://ACCOUNTINGINFO.COM

Between 1936 and 1946, the American Institute of Accountants established the Committee on Accounting Procedures (CAP). CAP was the first self-regulatory body for the accounting profession. CAP issued Accounting Research Bulletins (ARBs) to eliminate questionable accounting practices. Unfortunately, the ARBs did not establish an underlying theoretical framework for good accounting practices. In 1953, CAP began to establish generally accepted accounting procedures known as GAAP. GAAP are the structures and rules that accountants use to record and summarize transactions and to prepare financial statements. From this point, the standards-setting bodies evolved. In 1958, the Accounting Principles Board (APB) was created. The Financial Accounting Standards Board (FASB) was created in 1973[64] and was renamed the Accounting Standards Board (ASB) in 1990. If you have ever asked three different accountants the same question and received two different answers and a "Let me research that and get back to you," here is why. GAAP has evolved into an extremely complex set of standards, comprised of thousands of individual pronouncements issued by several accounting standards-setting bodies. There is no way any one accountant can be an expert in all aspects of accounting. Beginning in July 2009 and taking five years to complete, the FASB reorganized the U.S. GAAP catalog, including their 168 accounting pronouncements, into one centralized database for a single source of GAAP. The Codification Project included accounting literature by **all** of the standard setters. The Codification reorganized thousands of U.S. GAAP pronouncements into roughly 90 accounting topics and uses a consistent structure. The specifics of most of these standards are not immediately relevant to Information Technology, but select standards will be discussed later. The point here is the volumes of rules that have to be considered for the proper accounting treatment of each transaction and for each report that is issued.

These are the bodies that get to tell accountants what to do, where to go, how far to shove it, and the types of guidance they issue.

1. Financial Accounting Standards Board (FASB)
    a. Statements (FAS)
    b. Interpretations (FIN)
    c. Technical Bulletins (FTB)
    d. Staff Positions (FSP)
    e. Staff Implementation Guides (Q&A)
    f. Statement No. 138 Examples

2. Emerging Issues Task Force (EITF)
    a. Abstracts
    b. Topic D
3. Derivative Implementation Group (DIG) Issues
4. Accounting Principles Board (APB) Opinions
5. Accounting Research Bulletins (ARB)
6. Accounting Interpretations (AIN)
7. American Institute of Certified Public Accountants (AICPA)
    a. Statements of Position (SOP)
    b. Audit and Accounting Guides
    c. Practice Bulletins (PB)
    d. Technical Inquiry Service (TIS)

The Securities and Exchange Commission (SEC) issues accounting requirements and standards that become incorporated into GAAP. The most significant requirements related to the SEC include: Regulation S-X (SX), the regulation that dictates the specific format and content of financial reports; Financial Reporting Releases (FRR)/Accounting Series Releases (ASR), official guidelines and rules on all aspects of corporate accounting, including auditing policies and disclosure mandates; Interpretive Releases (IR) and SEC Staff guidance; and guidance on topics of general interest to the business and investment communities.[65]
And of course, we cannot forget Congress, the Internal Revenue Service, and the various state legislatures that can and often do claim jurisdiction over some aspect of financial reporting for companies.

GAAP standards are broad general statements that guide bookkeeping and and financial statement preparation. Financial statements prepared in accordance with GAAP are required for the release of those financial statements by publicly traded companies. Financial statements prepared using GAAP standards may also be mandated for privately-held companies, non-profit organizations, and governments. When GAAP is applied, it provides assurance to users of these statements that the reports are reliable.

Economic growth and its progression into a fully global economy have pushed the evolution of accounting and the co-opting of available information technology by accountants. Many international companies are doing business in the U.S., and many U.S. companies are doing business in foreign countries. International Financial Reporting Standards (IFRS) are developed by the International

Accounting Standards Board (IASB). IFRS are designed so that business affairs of companies are understandable and comparable across international boundaries. IFRS began as an effort to harmonize accounting practices across the European Union, and soon the value of globally comparable financial results became apparent. IFRS is gaining more and more acceptance. The countries that have currently adopted a version of IFRS that conforms to their specific needs are the European Union, Canada, Australia, India, Japan, Montenegro, Pakistan, Russia, Singapore, South Africa, Taiwan, and Turkey.

So, where does the U.S. stand on IFRS? While the SEC supports a common set of global accounting standards, full adoption of IFRS by U.S. companies is unlikely. In my opinion, the logical reasoning is that if the SEC forced U.S. companies to fully adopt IFRS, the SEC would be turning over a significant amount of control of U.S. companies to the international community. However, the SEC cannot reasonably expect companies to prepare financial statements in accordance with both U.S. GAAP and IFRS, which would be an unreasonable cost burden. The answer has to be convergence. In other words, as new accounting guidance and standards are needed, U.S. accounting standard setters will work jointly with the IASB to draft the standards. The first standard to be issued by a joint project of the

TITLE 26 OF US LAW, THE INTERNAL REVENUE CODE

FASB and the IASB is Revenue Recognition, which states how companies will record revenue. U.S. public companies will probably have to adopt this new standard in 2017. Implementation of this standard will have a major impact on the technology resources of a company.

As companies begin discussing the implementation of the new revenue recognition standards, you are now aware that there are forces at work greater than the accountants employed by your company. As systems are evaluated to determine the changes that are needed to ensure compliance, it will be imperative that the accountants be consulted before any changes are made and be kept in the loop as the projects progress.

I hope this discussion has given you an awareness of the massive body of knowledge that accountants are required to know. This is why many accountants specialize. We will soon see how this information relates to the structure of your Accounting department.

A fine is a tax for doing wrong.

A tax is a fine for doing well.[142]

CHAPTER 4
- FRIGGIN' BEAN COUNTERS -
WHO CARES WHAT THE NUMBERS ARE?

> *There are no accounting issues, no trading issues, no reserve issues, no previously unknown problem issues.*
>
> ~Kenneth Lay, an American businessman responsible for the corruption scandal that caused the collapse of Enron Corporation[66]

Every person, business, and government that earns and/or spends money needs accurate bookkeeping at a minimum. An accurate bookkeeping system can be as simple as a checkbook or as complex as a large ERP system. The end result of any bookkeeping and accounting system is to use transactional data to produce information in a meaningful format that is used to make decisions. It is important to understand who the potential end-users of the information generated are, to ensure that the accounting system selected is going to meet their needs.

People must manage their individual financial obligations, including household budgets and personal investments. They are responsible for accurate reporting of income to the Internal Revenue Service and if applicable, state and local taxation authorities. Examples of complete and accurate bookkeeping records include bank statements, wage statements, receipts, and checkbook registers. These records are essential for keeping the individual on target with their personal financial goals and keeping them out of jail for tax evasion. It is useful to note here, for your own education, there are two methods for not paying taxes. Those methods are tax avoidance and tax evasion. Tax avoidance is the use of any legal arrangement of one's financial affairs to minimize tax liability. Tax evasion is the deliberate under or non-payment of your tax liability. Practicing tax avoidance is rewarded with more money in your pocket; tax evasion means jail.

A business needs complete and accurate bookkeeping for the same reasons as individuals, but there has been an increase in the number of end-users requiring different types and levels of information. A business is an entity that utilizes resources to generate economic activity. A business entity can be arranged as a sole proprietorship, partnership or corporation, non-profit, or trust. Some of these entity arrangements can be publicly traded. Any company that is not publicly traded is said to be privately held. The type of business formed is a decision made by the owners, and several factors must be taken into consideration. These factors include but are not limited to the amount of individual risk an owner is willing to take, the ability to raise capital and obtain credit, and tax implications.

It is up to the business owners to determine the level of risk they are individually willing to take. In many situations, owners can be held personally liable for all acts of the business, including any acts by employees while "on the clock" and all financial obligations incurred.

Every Business Entity Needs to Count Beans

A sole proprietor is an individual acting on his or her own as a business. The sole proprietor generates revenue and incurs expenses. A sole proprietorship is the easiest business to form because, other than a business license issued by the authority where the business is located, no other filing or registrations are required. The primary drawback to operating as a sole proprietor is the owner is 100% liable for all of the business activity.

A partnership is formed when two or more individuals come together to form a business. Partnerships can be further classified as general partnerships or as limited liability partnerships. In a general partnership, the partners share in the liabilities of the partnership at some predetermined allocation. A limited liability partnership must have at least one general partner and at least one limited partner. The limited partner's liability is limited to their investment in the partnership. The partnership agreement can be in writing or verbal. The primary drawback to a partnership is that each partner can be held liable for the actions of the other partners as well as any employees. A partnership can leave the partners exposed to extensive liability.

A corporation is a separate legal entity from the owners. Corporations have most of the same rights and responsibilities as individuals, including the right to enter into contracts, loan and borrow money, sue and be sued, hire employees, own assets, and pay taxes. In other words, the corporation is liable for all of the business activity. Ownership of a corporation is evidenced by stock, making the stockholders the owners. Corporations can be privately held or publicly traded. A publicly traded corporation sells stock on a recognized stock exchange to the public, whereas a privately held corporation does not sell stock to the general public. Formation of a corporation is accomplished through legislation or a registration process established by state law and can be a complex and expensive undertaking.

Corporations can be classified as a C-corporation or S-corporation; these designations are strictly tax elections. Shareholders of a corporation elect how the corporation will be taxed under the United States Tax Code. If an S status is elected, the profits and losses flow through to the shareholders' personal tax returns, based on their ownership shares. A C status is a separate taxable entity.

Trusts and non-profits are also separate legal entities from the owners. They are formed for specific purposes. A trust is created to hold property subject to specific rules and safeguards for the benefit of others. A non-profit is an entity that utilizes surplus revenues to achieve its goals, usually charitable, rather than distributing the proceeds as dividends to owners or as tax payments to regulatory taxing authorities.

Governments are broadly defined as the administration of nations, states, and communities. Governments consume resources but typically do not generate economic activity. They do not generate revenue but instead collect taxes and user fees from the citizens to pay for the services provided. The main purposes of a government is to protect the citizens against the threat of internal and external attacks, create and enforce laws that preserve order, and provide services that benefit the whole, such as transportation infrastructure (public highways and airports), public primary education (grades kindergarten - 12th), and utilities (water, sewer, and trash).

Decision Makers Rely on Bean Counters

In addition to end-users of financial information, each of the entities described have stakeholders. Stakeholders are any party with an interest in the entity and include a variety of internal and external groups, individuals, and other entities. The interests could be the banker with an outstanding loan to the company, potential investors looking for a good return, environmental groups that are concerned about the company's "carbon footprint," taxation and other regulatory authorities, unions and other employee groups, the neighborhoods where the company operates, current employees, and the company's management. Stakeholders are decision makers that directly or indirectly influence operations by varying degrees of magnitude.

Internal decision makers include the board of directors; managers; employees; and in the case of sole proprietors and partnerships, the owners. This group makes decisions that have a direct impact on business operations. The magnitude of the decision's impact on the organization is usually dependent on the decision maker's position within the company. For example, the board of directors deciding to close a segment or to issue new stock will have a greater impact than a manager deciding to launch a new product line. The accounting staff deciding on the best accounting treatment for a transaction will have very little impact on business operations. However, decisions can have unintended consequences. The grocery store manager that decides to increase prices could greatly influence the decision of their customers to go to another store.

Regardless of the magnitude of the decision impact, all of these scenarios are equally dependent on reliable and accurate information for a positive outcome. Information produced for internal decision makers can be in any form that has meaning to the user and the decision at hand.

External decision makers can be direct or indirect. External direct decision makers are vendors, bankers, contractors, and customers. The decisions made by these groups can have varying degrees of significance to the company. A banker deciding on the creditworthiness of a company to finance a new product line can be significant. A vendor that decides credit terms or product pricing can have a profound impact on operations, depending on the relationship with the company.

For example, does the vendor supply significant components for manufacturing the company's products, or does it provide basic office supplies?

Companies that offer products and/or services that are necessary for everyday life, such as grocery stores or pest control, have millions of customers. The decisions made by individual customers probably have little impact on the operations of the company, such as a customer deciding a penny increase in price is too much to pay. However, a company with specialized products or services, such as aerospace or consulting, will also have a specialized customer base. Decisions made by these types of customers can have a major impact on the company.

External indirect decision makers could be institutional or individual investors. If the company is looking for a significant influx of capital, the institutional investors' decision could be significant; however, if the individual investor is trying to determine if the company's stock is a good investment through a recognized stock exchange, then their decision is going to have very little impact. These potential investors are the financial statement users for whom accounting standards have been developed.

Sometimes the decisions of internal and external decision makers can be interrelated with a wide range of potential consequences. How about the environmental group organizing a protest at a job site? The internal decision to ignore the environmental protest could lead to a damaged company reputation or government investigations.

The basic financial structure of every business, government, and non-profit is the same. They all have assets that include cash, liabilities, and owners' equity. As the

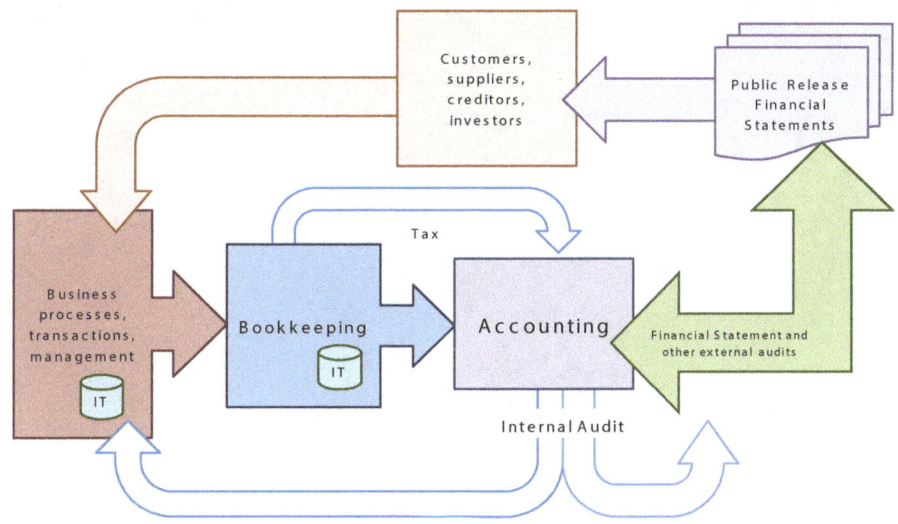

Basic accounting processes used by every business entity and how IT fits in

CHAPTER 4

basic accounting process figure above shows, the reporting needs of financial statement users can vary widely. Because of these varying needs, such as the banker granting credit and the investor looking to buy stock, it is important to know what the different accounting branches are and how they can best serve the users. The branch of accounting used will also determine the technology to be used.

A businessman was interviewing applicants for the position of divisional manager. He devised a simple test to select the most suitable person for the job. He asked each applicant the question, "What is two and two?" The first interviewee was a journalist. His answer was "Twenty-two." The second was a social worker. She said, "I don't know the answer but I'm glad we had time to discuss this important question." The third applicant was an engineer. He pulled out a slide rule and showed the answer to be between 3.999 and 4.001. The next person was a lawyer. He stated that in the case of Jenkins v. Commr of Stamp Duties (Qld), two and two was proven to be four. The last applicant was an accountant. The businessman asked him, "How much is two and two?" The accountant got up from his chair, went over to the door and closed it, then came back and sat down. He leaned across the desk and said in a low voice, "How much do you want it to be?" He got the job.[67]

CHAPTER 5

- FRIGGIN' BEAN COUNTERS -
FINANCE OR ACCOUNTING: WHO CARES

> *The great myth is the manager as orchestra conductor. It's this idea of standing on a pedestal and you wave your baton and accounting comes in, and you wave it somewhere else and marketing chimes in with accounting, and they all sound very glorious. But management is more like orchestra conducting during rehearsals, when everything is going wrong.*
>
> ~Henry Mintzberg (2009)[68]

Make no mistake, every event, transaction, and project occurring within a business will have an impact on the accounting of the business. There are many situations where you may find it necessary to solicit advice and/or assistance from your Accounting department. (I hope it will be standard procedure when you complete this book.) I realize that working with your accountants can be challenging. Because of the self-important flatulence of some accountants, it can be difficult to identify lines of authority and areas of responsibility. When undertaking projects, seeking advice on ROI, or looking for approvals to make a modification to the user interface of the accounting application, where do you go?

The department that handles the financial and reporting affairs of a business can be called Finance or Accounting. Some businesses use both terms interchangeably, and some organizations have two departments. Strictly speaking, Finance and Accounting are different functions that are dependent on each other. Finance is the management of assets and liabilities based on current information. Accounting manages the recording, reporting, and assessing of the financial transactions that have already occurred. In other words, Finance is looking to the future, while Accounting is analyzing the past.

There are no legal requirements that specify the name and structure of the department that handles the books and records and manages the finances of a company. The only requirement is that good control activities require segregation of duties (more later). The size and structure is dependent on the size and needs of the company. The names and structures vary from company to company and are usually influenced by the backgrounds of the owners or employees building the functions.

If an organization has a Finance department, it is usually an all-encompassing term that includes Accounting. The largest global organizations often have multiple Finance and Accounting departments that are established in strategically significant geographic locations, often influenced by domestic and international regulatory reporting requirements. Small and medium companies usually have an Accounting department that also performs the tasks associated with a Finance department.

The Places Beans Are Counted - Typical Finance Functions within a Business

Finance is closely related to accounting. The primary function of finance is the allocation of assets and liabilities over time. Finance applies economic theories and has been defined as the science of money management and the joy of financial security. To give you a frame of reference when attempting to obtain information, the following list provides a brief description of what each department does.

- Treasury - The function that manages cash flows to ensure that daily operating needs are met and to generate the most profitable returns on excess cash. Treasury also forecasts future cash needs and determines the best alternatives for obtaining cash when current operating cash flow is not sufficient.
    - Cash Management - A broad area of finance usually performed within Treasury. Cash management typically manages the collection, investing and the use of cash.
    - Debt Service - Management of the cash requirements during a specific time period to repay interest and principal on business debts.
- Financial Planning and Analysis (FP&A) - The function that is responsible for preparing budgets and forecasts in accordance with the company's budgeting processes and procedures. FP&A is generally responsible for preparing internal management reports and analysis on everything, including proposed projects, budget to actual variance analysis, and due diligence for mergers and acquisitions.
    - Budgeting - The estimation of revenue and expenses over a future time period, usually a year. The process begins with historical results from the accounting system. Known events, organizational goals and objectives, and management expectations are considered when establishing a budget.
    - Financial Analysis - The process of evaluating projects, budgets, and other related activities to determine potential suitability and to determine the stability, solvency, liquidity, and profitability of the business.
- Mergers and Acquisitions (M&A) - The function that considers the risks and rewards related to the consolidation of companies by using due diligence and other analytical techniques. A merger occurs when

two companies combine to form a new company; an acquisition is the purchase of one company by another.

- ▲ Due Diligence - An investigation or audit of a potential investment. The investment could be the purchase of a company or a simpler type of investment. Due diligence attempts to confirm all material facts in a sale or purchase. Due diligence is a legal concept that refers to the care a reasonable person should take before entering into a transaction with another party.

More Places Where Beans Are Counted - Typical Accounting Functions within a Business

The Accounting department can be a scary and mysterious department to deal with. Typically the most contact you have had with Accounting was the Accounts Payable department. They would be the department that makes sure your suppliers are paid and that your expense report is paid. Hopefully, the following brief descriptions will give you a roadmap to decode the mystery.

- Accounts Payable (AP) - The function within accounting that is responsible for recording expenses and making payments owed by the company to suppliers and other creditors. A large company may assign the issuing of checks to the Treasury or Cash-Management function.

- Accounts Receivable (AR) - The function within accounting that manages the record keeping for customers that owe the company for goods or services that have been delivered but not paid for. Trade receivables usually come in the form of credit lines that have been granted to customers based on the company's credit-granting policies. AR is usually settled within a short time period, ranging from a few days to a year.

- General Ledger (GL) - The function within accounting that maintains the company's main accounting record(s).

- Payroll (PR) - The function within accounting that ensures that the company's employees are paid correctly, in the appropriate intervals, and within any regulatory requirements.

- Tax - The function within accounting that manages the company's regulatory tax liabilities and any audits performed by the taxing authorities.

- Financial Reporting - The function within accounting that prepares all reports for external reporting.

Both Accounting and Finance require staff with some level of specialized training. Staffing levels depend on the size of the department and the distribution of work. A qualified accounting or finance professional could supervise both Accounting and Finance staff that perform multiple functions, such as tax accounting, financial reporting, and payroll. Companies are free to structure their Accounting and Finance departments, including staff titles and reporting relationships in any way that makes sense to their business.

There is significant confusion about the difference and the relevance of accountancy, accounting, accountants, certified public accountants, bookkeepers, and auditors. How do you know what is what, how does any of this relate to Information Technology, and most important, why should you care? I am going to tell you.

Principles of Accountancy, American Bookkeeping Series, a textbook written by Lloyd E. Goodyear in 1913[69], gives some great definitions that are still relevant today. Some key words in these definitions highlight and build the relationship between accounting and information technology:

1. Accountancy - The branch of **mathematical science** that treats the **relations of values expressible in terms of money.** It is useful in discovering the causes of business success and failures. The principles of accountancy are applied to business concerns in three divisions of practical art: accounting, bookkeeping, and auditing.

2. Accounting - The art of exhibiting the component parts of a business organization through their own expression in accounts, which are formed, continued, and closed in accordance with a body of governing principles outlined in the course of centuries of progress in accountancy. An accountant arranges and prepares a bookkeeping system adapted to the needs of a given business and derives from the system an accumulation of guiding facts for the benefit of the business organization. The accountant is the architect of the bookkeeping structure.

3. Bookkeeping - The art of **recording business transactions** and operations. There are two principal phases of bookkeeping: (1) the preservation of a true business history of some certain concern; and (2) the classification of the items recorded in such a way as to show the receipts and disbursements of cash and the cost and yield of the other component parts of a given concern. A bookkeeper should know: (1) how to record all transactions that occur in a given business; (2) how to post all entries to the proper accounts; (3) how to show the condition of any account by means of a statement; (4) how to verify his work through a trial balance; and (5) how to preserve vouchers relating to the records.

4. Auditing - The art of examining books, records, accounts, and the

business interests with a view to discovering the actual condition. An auditor is employed, ordinarily: (1) to detect fraud; (2) to prove the mechanical and mathematical accuracy of books; (3) to discover points in which the books do not conform to the principles of accountancy; (4) to exhibit the true condition of a business; and (5) to make recommendations with a view to improvement.[70]

Note the important differences in the definitions of accounting and bookkeeping. With today's technology, bookkeeper and bookkeeping have become an obsolete title and job function. In today's ERP environments, there is very little distinction between bookkeeper and bookkeeping and accountant and accounting. A bookkeeper performs the recording of financial transactions. The accountant creates any necessary reports from the financial transactions recorded by the bookkeeper and files any necessary forms with government agencies. Bookkeeping is a function of accounting, but in a historical sense, accounting is not a function of bookkeeping.

An accountant visited the natural history museum. While standing near a T-Rex skeleton he said to his neighbor:

"This dinosaur is two billion years and ten months old,"

"Where did you get this exact information?"

"I was here 10 months ago and the guide said the dinosaur is two billion years old.[71]"

CHAPTER 6

– FRIGGIN' BEAN COUNTERS – ISN'T IT ALL COUNTING BEANS?

> *I know what I don't know. To this day, I don't know technology,
> and I don't know finance or accounting.*
>
> ~**Bernard Ebbers**[72]

Accounting is a dynamic profession that adapts to the specific and varying needs of decision makers and other users of transactional information. Accountancy has branched out into different types of accounting to satisfy the diverse information needs of decision makers.

Financial accounting is the process of recording, summarizing, and reporting business transactions to provide accurate reporting of the company's financial position and performance. The primary objective of financial accounting is the preparation of financial statements.[73] The types or methods of accounting a company can use are referred to as "bases." There are several comprehensive bases of accounting that can be used by a company. The accrual basis is GAAP and is the primary requirement for financial statements that are going to be issued to the public. The accrual basis of accounting measures economic events rather than the movement of cash. The idea is to match revenue to the expense incurred to generate that revenue at the time the transaction occurs; for example, the sale of widgets is recorded with the costs to acquire or produce the widgets. U.S. companies that have stock bought and sold on a public exchange are required to use accrual basis for financial reporting.

Other comprehensive bases of accounting (OCBOA) are methods that are not considered GAAP, but they may be required by regulatory requirements or internal business needs. OCBOA methods that a company can use for financial statement preparation include:

- Cash Basis - Measures income and expenses only when cash is received (income) and the bills are paid (expense). This is the method used by most individuals.

- Modified Cash Basis - Is a hybrid of the accrual basis and cash basis. Generally, income is recognized when cash is received and expenses are recognized when incurred. This method is used by many governments.

- Income Tax Basis - Accounting for tax implications that affect the business. Tax accounting must conform to rules and laws of the jurisdictions the company operates in. Tax matters include international, federal, state, and local income taxes; sales and use taxes; property taxes; and any other potential tax implications. Tax accounting rules can differ significantly from GAAP.

- Statutory Basis - Used when required by an enforcement agency for a regulated industry. Currently, it is required by the National Association of Insurance Commissioners for the preparation of insurance company financial statements.

Management accounting produces information for internal use by the company's management. The information is more detailed than the financial statements produced for publication. The intent is to provide internal decision makers with enough detail to effectively control, plan, and meet the organizational objectives and strategic plan. The form and content of the reports produced is determined by the needs of management.

Cost accounting, also known as project or process accounting and job costing, is a specific form of management accounting. The primary purpose is to use the accounting system to monitor and control costs and to track the financial progress of projects. Cost accounting is used in project-oriented businesses such as manufacturing and construction. Many companies also use cost accounting to track the costs of internally developed fixed assets. Other forms of cost accounting are production and activity based accounting. Production accounting is a specialized form of project accounting. The primary purpose is to track the production costs of filming individual movies and television episodes. Activity-based Costing is a specialized form of cost accounting that identifies business activities and then assigns the indirect cost to products, recognizing the relationship between costs, activities, and products.

Fund accounting is used by governments and non-profit entities. A fund is a set of accounts established for specific purposes in accordance with laws, regulations, or special restrictions. A government or non-profit will have multiple funds in the accounting records. The purpose of the fund dictates the accounting basis that is used. The general fund is the primary accounting record by governments for taxes received and expenditures made with those taxes. The basis of accounting used for the general fund is the modified cash basis. If a government operates a souvenir stand at a park, then the basis of accounting used for that fund may be the accrual basis. The need for separate funds is to emphasize accountability rather than profitability. Financial constraints on the use of resources are often imposed. Fund accounting ensures that the financial position and performance of a fund is set within a budgetary context. Separate rules are established and followed in many jurisdictions to account for the transactions and events in funds.

There are specialized areas of accounting. Forensic accounting involves fraud and embezzlement investigative techniques using accounting and auditing to analyze financial information. Actuarial accounting utilizes statistical methods to evaluate the probability of events occurring and to quantify contingent outcomes. The main focus is to minimize the impacts of financial losses associated with undesirable events. Forensic and actuarial accounting are most often utilized by insurance companies and pension administrators. Social accounting or corporate social responsibility reporting and sustainability accounting, is the newest branch of accounting and is used for reporting the impact of business activities on the ecological and social environment.

Any combination of these branches of accounting can exist in your organization, and they all use the same transactional information from the accounting system. However, the form and format of the information produced is going to be different for each branch.

Did you hear about the accounting program that can do everything an accountant can do and crack jokes?

CHAPTER 7

- FRIGGIN' BEAN COUNTERS - WHO NEEDS 'EM?

An accountant is a man who watches the battle from the safety of the hills and then comes down to bayonet the wounded.[75]

Meet the Bean Counters - The Accountants

Just as the size and structure of the Accounting department is dependent on the size and needs of the company, the staffing required is dependent on the size of the department. The challenge for those outside the Accounting department is to identify the proper lines of authority, the best staff to assist with proper functionality of the accounting application, and the appropriate accounting individuals to consult on projects.

Typical financial management titles include chief financial officer (CFO), chief accounting officer (CAO), vice president of finance, vice president of financial reporting, vice president of financial planning and analysis, vice president of tax, controller, assistant controller, and accounting manager. To qualify for any of these titles generally requires a finance or accounting degree and a significant amount of prior experience. The support staff consists of various educational and skill levels. The general job description and education requirements stated here are for comparative purposes and to provide a basis for understanding the different positions within the Accounting department.

The primary responsibility for the oversight of the company finances falls to the CFO. The CFO may or may not be an accountant by training, but at a minimum will have specialized knowledge about the company and expertise in financial matters. In smaller companies, the controller may have the role of the CFO. The CFO reports directly to the chief executive officer (CEO). The CEO is the top position in an organization. The CEO's main responsibility is developing and implementing high-level strategies, oversight of operations and resources, and acting as liaison between the board of directors and the company staff.

A company that is publicly traded is required to have a board of directors (BOD). The board of directors is a group of individuals who are elected by and to act as representatives of the stockholders. The BOD is charged with oversight of the company and has the authority to hire and fire the CEO and to make policies and decisions around major issues. Major issues that require board of director action include, but are not limited to, declaring dividends, setting policies for stock options, determining executive compensation, and establishing an audit and compensation committee. The CEO of a public company reports directly to the BOD. The CEO will often have a position on the board, and in some cases is the chairperson. If the company is privately held, the CEO may be the top of the hierarchy without BOD oversight.

The CFO will hire trained and qualified accounting and finance professionals to run the day-to-day accounting operations. Large companies could have multiple Accounting departments with multiple layers of accounting management. If Accounting departments are geographically disbursed, each location will have qualified accounting management.

In many cases, multiple levels of accounting management become necessary because of inefficiencies in the accounting application implementation. Implementing multiple manual interventions in response to a badly implemented ERP will create the need for additional staff and management. For example, if the interface from the production system does not map to the general ledger, a staff accountant may be needed to ensure the manual download and upload of the data is accurate and complete.

Basic accounting job responsibilities, education, and skill levels include:

- CFO – Responsible for all finance and accounting functions, including drafting and instituting all internal accounting policies and procedures, internal and external financial reporting, income tax return preparation and planning, managing the treasury function, obtaining financing for planned acquisitions, and maintaining a positive cash flow for the company. The CFO generally has a high level of education and/or industry experience.

- Controller – Responsible for the day-to-day accounting processes, including the accurate and timely recording of all financial transactions. This includes supervising the monthly, quarterly, and annual accounting close processes, maintaining a review process for monitoring the accuracy of the data used for financial reporting, creating and monitoring deadlines for timely reporting, monitoring adherence to internal accounting policies and procedures, and assisting all users of financial information. The controller generally has a high level of accounting or finance education, along with significant industry experience, and often has achieved the professional designation of CPA. Depending on the size and structure of the company, the job role could be responsible for both the CFO and controller duties.

- Assistant Controller/Accounting Manager – Responsible for recording both balance sheet and income statement transactions and the monthly accounting close process. This includes a monthly comparison of actual to budgeted results and investigating major variances. The assistant controller/accounting manager also supervises the work of senior and staff accountants. The assistant controller/accounting manager has a high level of accounting or finance education but less industry experience than the controller. He or she may have just earned or is in the process of earning the CPA designation. If a company has both assistant controllers and accounting managers, the accounting manager will report to the assistant controller. The accounting manager could also be called the accounting supervisor. If all three titles exist, the accounting supervisor will report to the accounting manager.

- Senior Accountant – Responsible for recording both balance sheet and income statement transactions and the monthly accounting close process. The senior accountants will typically supervise the work of staff accountants, and accounts payable and accounts receivable personnel. They also ensure that all balance sheet accounts are accurately stated and supported to validate the accuracy and completeness of the financial general ledger transactions. The senior accountant has accounting education but has limited accounting or industry experience and may have just achieved or is working on the CPA designation.

- Staff Accountant - Responsible for recording both balance sheet and income statement transactions and the monthly accounting close process. The staff accountant may be a recent graduate with no industry experience.

- Accounting Clerk - Generally an entry-level support position for the Accounting department that performs routine tasks, such as posting cash and filing. The accounting clerk has limited accounting or finance education.

- Accounts Payable (AP) (Manager, Supervisor, Staff, Clerk) – Responsible for the processing of supplier or vendor invoices for payment. This includes verifying that each invoice was properly approved and is mathematically accurate, duplicate invoices are not processed, and late fees are avoided. AP staff generally do not have or has limited accounting or finance education. They may have earned their roles through experience, vocational training, or in-house training programs.

- Accounts Receivable (AR) (Supervisor, Staff, Clerk) - Responsible for the day-to-day recording of revenue transactions, billing, and applying payments to customer accounts, and the collection of past due accounts. AR staff generally do not have or have limited accounting or finance education. They achieve their roles through experience, vocational training, or in-house training programs. The following can report to Accounting, Finance or have a separate reporting structure, depending on the organization:

- Vice President of Tax - Responsible for tax compliance with all taxing authorities. The vice president of tax generally has a high level of accounting education with a specialty in taxation, significant industry experience, and significant experience communicating with taxation authorities.

- Tax Accountant - Primarily responsible for adjusting the financial statements prepared under financial accounting principles to account for the differences with tax laws. The purpose is to compile information that can be used for tax planning and to estimate tax liabilities.

- Forensic Accountant - Has expertise in using accounting and audit techniques to assess the financial effects of a loss or to detect financial fraud. Forensic accountants have a high level of accounting education and investigative education and/or experience. The forensic accountant differs from internal auditors, which will be addressed in detail later.

- Cost Accountant – Has expertise in management accounting and is an expert at tracking costs associated with specific projects. The cost accountant has a high level of accounting education and industry experience.

- Project Accountant - Has expertise in accounting for projects and a high level of accounting education or experience.

- Fund Accountant - Has expertise in accounting for governments and non-profit entities. Fund accountants have a high level of accounting education and experience.

Basic finance job responsibilities, education, and skill levels include:

- Vice President of Finance - Responsible for all functions related to the finance function. The vice president for finance generally has a high level of finance education and extensive industry experience.

- Vice President of FP&A - Responsible for all functions related to financial planning and budgeting, usually including merger and acquisition activities. The vice president of FP&A generally has a high level of finance education and extensive industry experience.

- Treasurer – Responsible for signing checks and setting up wire transfers within the company's established limits, setting up recurring wires, executing replacement reserve processes, making payments of notes payable, establishing bank accounts and bank relationships, and managing cash. The treasurer is also responsible for supervising the assistant treasurer and other treasury staff. The treasurer has a high level of education in finance or accounting and/or significant experience in the industry and dealing with financial institutions.
- Assistant Treasurer – Responsible for making all notes payable and reporting, and assisting the treasurer with cash management, wire, and other banking functions. The assistant treasurer has education in finance or accounting, with less experience than the treasurer.

Now that we understand the structure of the Accounting department and the accountants that perform the bookkeeping functions and prepare financial information, we can examine the actual mechanics of bookkeeping and accounting.

HERE ARE THE TOP 10 REASONS TO BECOME AN ACCOUNTANT:

10. Audits happen
9. You're too sincere to succeed in marketing
8. You can take your "stupid accounting tricks" with you when you change jobs
7. Pocket protectors are bound to come back in style
6. You get to see your old friends every six months at the CPA exam
5. Business Administration majors go to work for their parents
4. Norm Peterson makes a great role model
3. You can color your conversations with exciting phrases like "alternative minimum tax" and "substantive tests of details"
2. You have great pick-up lines for parties: "Hey baby, can I vouch your assets?"
1. You don't have to go to law school to get a job!

CHAPTER 7

CHAPTER 8

- FRIGGIN' BEAN COUNTERS -
DOUBLE ENTRY DOUBLE TALK

If you can't explain it simply, you don't understand it well enough.

~ ALBERT EINSTEIN[77]

Since the second generation of computers and the introduction of assembly language, the bookkeeping function has gradually become more automated. Bookkeeping is a systematic, repeatable process that follows a predefined set of rules, which makes it a perfect candidate for automation. We can say that the computer killed the bookkeeper, making it important for the IT professional to at least be aware of the basic concepts of double-entry bookkeeping. A basic understanding of the bookkeeping process will go a long way in helping the IT professional properly support the accounting applications, including troubleshooting issues and providing guidance with end-user configurations.

Prior to the publication of *Summa de Arithmetic, Geometria, Proportioni et Proportionalita* by Pacioli, describing double-entry bookkeeping, accounting records were simple lists. This was the bookkeeping method used by the farmers and merchants of Babylon and ancient Greece. The primary purpose of these lists was to serve as memory aides. Even today, the primary bookkeeping record for most individuals and sole proprietors is a single list of transactions known as a checkbook. The checkbook contains entries that represent amounts paid, such as utility bills, and amounts earned, such as wages. The larger a business grows, the more transactions it has to process and track and the more sophisticated the bookkeeping records need to be.

The Many Essential Elements of the Bookkeeping System Needed to Count Beans

Bookkeeping is the recording of financial transactions, and is part of the accounting process. The common methods of bookkeeping are single-entry, keeping a checkbook, and double-entry, which is the method used by most businesses. The double-entry system is an involved process. The basic elements needed for any double-entry system include:

- Chart of Accounts - The list of accounts used to categorize each class of transactions for which money or the equivalent is spent or received. It is used to organize the finances and to identify expenditures, revenue, assets, liabilities, and owners' equity.

- Journals or Day Books - Books of original entry that are descriptive and chronological (diary-like) records of day-to-day financial transactions. The journal details must be entered formally to enable posting to ledgers. Journals can be designed to meet the particular needs of the business. Typical journals include:

- ▲ Cash Book - Original entries for cash receipts and cash payments.
- ▲ Merchandise Sold Book - Original entries of the merchandise sold, listed item by item.
- ▲ Merchandise Bought Book - Original entries of all merchandise purchased for resale or in-house use.
- ▲ Account Sales Register - Original entries of sales made to customers that have been granted credit terms.

• Ledger - A detailed record showing beginning and ending balances and all of the increases and decreases affecting those balances. The different ledgers are:

- ▲ General Ledger - Captures summary business activity for each account listed in the chart of accounts.
- ▲ Sales or Accounts Receivable Ledger - Consists of individual ledger records that keep a running total of activity by customer for those that have been granted credit terms. Also called a subsidiary ledger that supports in detail the general ledger accounts receivable balance. All individual customer ledgers with a balance must total to the general ledger accounts receivable balance.
- ▲ Purchase Ledger - Consists of purchasing transactions needed to operate the business. Individual supplier or vendor ledgers are maintained to keep a running total of the money owed to each. Also called a subsidiary ledger that supports in detail the general ledger accounts payable balance.
- ▲ Payroll Ledger - Consists of individual ledger records that keep a running total of all payroll activity by employee. Also called a subsidiary ledger that supports in detail all of the general ledger payroll-related account balances.

• Trial Balance - A bookkeeping worksheet that compiles the ending balances of all general ledger accounts. The trial balance is prepared on a periodic basis to ensure that the bookkeeping system is mathematically correct. All debits must equal all credits so that the trial balance equals zero. The trial balance in provided to the accountant and is the starting point for financial statement preparation.

Bookkeeping rules for books of original entry state that every transaction must have the following essential elements: the date of transaction, the person with whom the company transacts, the details of the transaction, the transaction amounts, and the ledger accounts to which the transaction will be posted. All bookkeeping entries are made to show the effects of transactions upon the business.[78]

The double-entry bookkeeping system is a set of rules for recording financial transactions. According to the *Principles of Accountancy, American Bookkeeping Series,* the original entries are made at the time the transaction occurs and serve as the basis for the amounts transferred to the ledger accounts. The original entry must record the transaction facts and the ledger accounts affected. The day books or journals are used to record all transaction facts by listing them in order of occurrence. At the end of the day, transactions written in the journals are summarized to provide information used for posting to the general ledger. Every transaction recorded in the general ledger has at least one debit and one credit entry.[79]

To Keep the Bean Counts Accurate: Nine Steps of the Bookkeeping Cycle

The bookkeeping or accounting cycle is the term used to describe the collective process of recording and processing the accounting events. The steps begin when a transaction occurs and end with the transaction's inclusion in the financial statements.

1. Collecting and analyzing data from transactions and events.
2. Putting transactions into the appropriate journal.
3. Posting entries to the general ledger.
4. Preparing an unadjusted trial balance.
5. Adjusting entries appropriately.
6. Preparing an adjusted trial balance.
7. Organizing the accounts into the financial statements.
8. Closing the books.
9. Preparing a post-closing trial balance to check the accounts.[80]

Following this set of rules ensures the accuracy and conformity of financial statements. Computerized accounting systems have helped reduce mathematical and posting errors in the cycle. Prior to computerized accounting, steps 1–4 were basic double-entry bookkeeping done by bookkeepers. Steps 5–9 were typically done by accountants.

Counting the Beans for the Sales at Grandpa Otis' General Store

Grandpa Otis' POS system

Manual Bookkeeping Journals/Ledgers

Consider a local general store, family-owned and operated by Grandpa Otis in Small Town USA prior to the 1970s. The bookkeeping for a typical day's operation would consist of the manual recording of each transaction in multiple journals as they occurred. To properly track sales and other business activity, Grandpa Otis has a cash register and adding machine, journals for writing down transactions, a checkbook, and several pens and pencils. The journals next to the register are

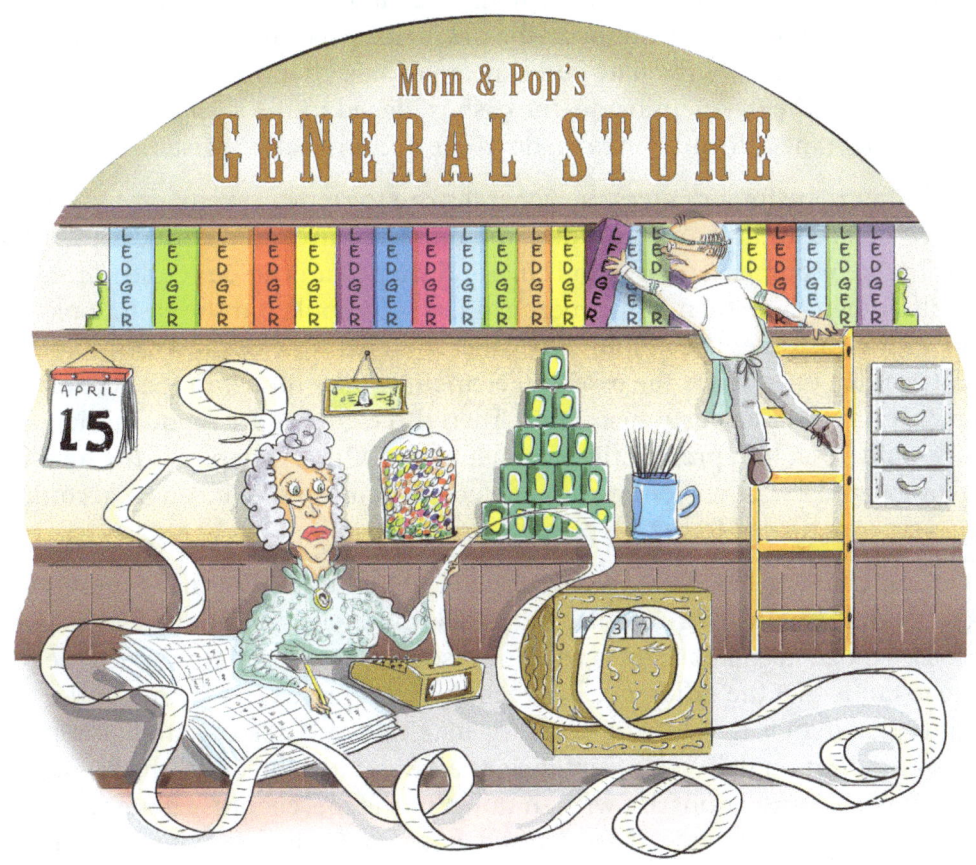

the cash, sales on account, and the merchandise sold. Grandpa Otis is a kindly old storekeeper, carries a variety of inventory for resale, and has established house accounts for many customers. He also has a generous return policy.

A day begins with a customer making a cash purchase. Grandpa Otis writes the essential elements of the transaction, including merchandise and the selling price, in the merchandise sold book. The prices are added up and a total is presented to the customer. The customer pays cash for the merchandise. The cash received is written in the cash book, placed in the cash drawer, and change is given to the customer.

The next customer buys merchandise on account. Grandpa Otis will write down all the merchandise and related selling prices in the merchandise sold book and give the customer a receipt to sign. This time, the essential elements of the transaction are also written in the account sales register. The essential elements include the customer to receive the invoice at the end of the month, what was purchased, the amount purchased on account, and the date and time.

Another customer comes in to make a cash payment for a prior month's sales on account. Grandpa Otis will write the essential elements of the transaction in the cash book, including who made the payment, what the payment was for, the payment amount, and the date and time, to ensure that the customer receives proper credit for the payment made, the cash is placed in the cash drawer, and an entry with the same information is made in the account sales register.

The next customer enters the general store to return two items. One was purchased on account the previous day, and one was purchased with cash the prior month. The item purchased for cash is in good shape and can be resold. Grandpa Otis writes down the return in the merchandise sold book and the cash book, and then gives the customer the money. The other item has a defect and cannot be resold. Grandpa Otis writes the essential elements of the return in the account sales register to give the customer credit. Then three entries are made in the merchandise sold book to represent the returned items. One entry places the item back in inventory, and the other removes the defective item, so that it can be accounted for as waste or returned to the supplier for credit.

Grandpa Otis has done an amazing job of building a popular general store. He is constantly buying merchandise to restock the shelves. Grandpa Otis is cost conscious, a tough negotiator, and is winning discounts to pass on to his customers. He understands that the difference between the sales price of an item and the cost to acquire that item is the starting point for making a profit, so accurate bookkeeping is essential. Upon delivery acceptance, the essential elements of the merchandise purchasing transactions are written down in the merchandise bought book, including the supplier's name, date received, a description of each item, whether it was purchased for resale or for use in the store, and the cost. There will also be a notation made regarding whether or not the items were purchased on account and if a check was written or cash was paid at the time of delivery. If a check was written to pay for the merchandise at delivery, the essential elements are written in the checkbook. If cash is taken out of the register, a negative entry is written in the cash book with all of the essential elements.

Consider each transaction described above occurring multiple times per day, with each being arduously manually recorded in multiple journals in the same manner. At the end of the day, the books have to be balanced. The merchandise sold book, cash book, and account sales register are totaled. The total activity in the merchandise sold book represents the day's sales. The combined totals in the cash book and the account sales register must equal the total of the merchandise sold book. If the totals do not equal, transactions are missing or were written down incorrectly. The transactions have to be identified and corrected before the daily activity can be closed. When the daily cash book total plus the daily total of the account sales register equals the daily total of the merchandise sold book, the cash can be counted. The actual cash in the cash drawer must equal the cash written down in the cash book. If the totals do not match, the missing or incorrect transactions must be identified and corrected or the missing money must be found. When the cash on hand equals the cash book, the cash is deposited in the bank. The "balanced" journals are then given to the bookkeeper. Phew! You might think you are done, but in reality, the daily bookkeeping is only half done.

After working all day in the home taking care of the children, Grandma Otis switches aprons and becomes the bookkeeper for the general store. The primary responsibility of the bookkeeper is to take the transactions from the journals, summarize them, and record them in the correct general ledger accounts. Grandma Otis starts with posting. The posting process involves taking the day's transactions written in the journals and summarizing them into journal entries to be posted (written down) in the general ledger. To say a transaction has been posted to the general ledger also means that the transaction has been recorded. The most efficient way to record transactions to the general ledger is to prepare a journal entry for each transaction. A debit or credit entry will be made to each general ledger account affected by the day's transactions. The accounts in the general ledger consist of real and nominal accounts. Real accounts include cash and any account that has a cash value either owed to or owed by the business.

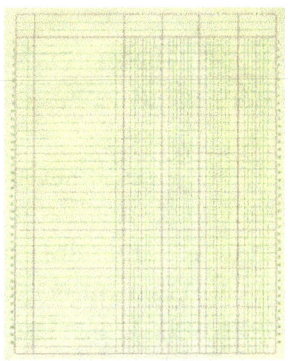

Ledger Paper, Grandma Otis' Spreadsheet

These are the accounts that make up the balance sheet. Nominal accounts are temporary accounts. These accounts are closed or "zeroed" at the end of each year. Income statement accounts are nominal accounts and are used to determine profit or loss for the business. Accounts in the general ledger are broadly classified as assets, liabilities, equity, income, and expenses. Assets and expenses have a normal debit balance, represented as a positive number. To increase the balance of an asset

	Account Classification	Normal Balance	Increase	Decrease
Real Accounts	Assets	+	+	-
	Liabilities	-	-	+
	Owner's Equity	-	-	+
Nominal Accounts	Income	-	-	+
	Expense	+	+	-

NORMAL ACCOUNT BALANCES AND HOW DEBITS (+) AND CREDITS (-) IMPACT REAL AND NOMINAL ACCOUNTS

or expense, you record a debit entry. To reduce the balance, a credit entry is necessary. Liabilities, income, and equity have a normal credit balance, represented as a negative number. To increase the balance of a liability, income, or equity account, a credit entry is needed. To reduce a liability, income, or equity balance, a debit is recorded.

The chart of accounts for the general store is simple. The following accounts are sufficient to capture all of the activity and produce meaningful financial statements.

Grandma Otis starts with the account sales register. Each customer with a house account has an individual ledger card to track their individual transactions in detail. The sales on account transactions are recorded to each affected ledger card. When complete, the total sales activity for the day that is recorded to the individual ledgers must equal the account sales register. Journal entry number 1 is prepared for posting the total sales from the account sales register to the accounts receivable general ledger account as a debit, with a credit made to sales.

Grandma Otis will then prepare the cash entry from the cash book for posting to the general ledger. Payments made by house account customers are posted to the correct customer ledger, and then each ledger card is totaled for an ending balance by customer. Once this is complete, journal entry number 2 is prepared to debit cash for the total cash received for the day and credit the accounts

Account Number	Description	Classification
10	Cash	Assets
20	Accounts Receivable	
25	Allowance for Doubtful Accounts	
30	Inventory	
40	Property Plant and Equipment	
45	Accumulated Depreciation	
50	Accounts Payable	Liabilities
60	Owner's Equity	Equity
70	Sales	Revenue
75	Sales Returns and Allowance	
80	Cost of Goods Sold	Cost of Goods
90	Payroll	Operating Expenses
100	Supplies	
105	Bad Debt Expense	
110	Other Expenses	

GENERAL STORE CHART OF ACCOUNTS. IN A MANUAL BOOKKEEPING SYSTEM, THESE ACCOUNTS CAPTURE SUFFICIENT TRANSACTION ACTIVITY TO GENERATE FINANCIAL STATEMENTS.

receivable general ledger account for the amount paid on account. The sales revenue account is also credited for the balance of cash sales. When the posting is complete, the total ending balance of all house account ledgers **must** equal the accounts receivable general ledger and the total debit to the cash account in the general ledger must equal the deposit to the bank.

    To summarize, the impact of journal entry 1 is to increase the accounts receivable general ledger account and to increase revenue by the sales on account. Journal entry 2 reduces the accounts receivable accounts by the payments made, increases cash, and increases revenue. Revenue is an income statement nominal account with a normal credit balance. Cash and accounts receivable are assets with normal debit balances and are real accounts. The accounts receivable general ledger account is also known as the control account and represents the total amount of money the house account customers owe the general store. Each individual customer ledger, collectively known as a subsidiary ledger, supports the balance of accounts receivable by stating which customer owes how much. The cash general ledger account represents the amount of money (actual cash) the general store has. The cash account is supported by the monthly bank reconciliation.

    To complete the journal entries for the daily sales activities, Grandma Otis will take the merchandise sold book and find the original cost of each item sold to compute the cost of goods sold. The original cost is multiplied by the number of items sold and then totaled. Journal entry number 3 is prepared for the original cost of the merchandise sold as a debit to the cost of goods sold and a credit to the inventory account. Inventory is an asset and a real account with a normal debit balance; a credit entry reduces the inventory balance. Cost of goods sold is an expense and a nominal account with a normal debit balance. If the general store sold 1,000 items, Grandma Otis would be looking up the original cost of each item, either by reviewing prior entries in the merchandise bought book or the actual vendor invoice.

You could make the argument that Grandma Otis can record cost of sales once a month by doing a physical inventory count. However, the cost of individual items would still have to be looked up to ensure the cost of goods sold is properly calculated. Either method is valid, but if you follow Pacioli's rule #3 of what every businessman needs, "an accounting system which allows him to view his finances at a glance," then you want to record cost of sales daily.

Grandma Otis proceeds to post each journal entry, which collectively function as a summary of the daily transactions, to the corresponding general ledger accounts. After recording each journal entry, a check mark is written to ensure that the journal entry is not recorded twice. After posting, Grandma Otis notices that the total cash posted as a debit to the general ledger account does not equal the amount Grandpa Otis deposited in the bank. Grandma Otis must go back and determine the reason the cash does not equal the bank deposit. Remember the customer that returned the merchandise? Grandpa Otis did not make the transaction's essential elements very clear. The amount of cash refunded to the customer was included in the entry to record cash taken in. Grandma Otis prepares journal entry 4 to correct the daily activity. One error made in summarizing and posting generates two entries to correct it.

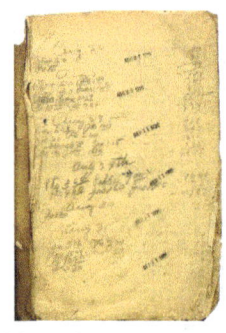

Messy Ledger in a manual bookkeeping system

The returned item that was sold in a previous month should not affect the current daily sales. To account for these types of returns, contra accounts are used. The purpose of a contra account is to track activity that is "contra" to the normal account activity. The sales return & allowances account is a "contra" revenue and nominal account with a normal debit balance; the related sales account has a normal credit balance. Other contra accounts are allowance for doubtful accounts, which is related to accounts receivable and accumulated depreciation accounts for each property plant and equipment account. When the financial statements are prepared, the contra accounts are combined with the related account into one line item and presented on the appropriate report, either the income statement or the balance sheet.

The final sales-related entry Grandma Otis makes is for the merchandise returned for the current period. She records the return to the customer ledger, giving the proper credit, and then she prepares journal entry number 5 for posting to the general ledger.

		Grandpa Otis General Store					Initials	Date
		Journal Entries for xx/xx/19xx			Prepared by		G.O.	xx
					Approved by			

JE#	DATE	Account	Description	✓	DEBIT (+)		CREDIT (−)	
1	xx/xx/19xx	20	Accounts Receivalbe	✓	xxxx	00		
		70	Sales				xxxx	00
			To record sales to house accounts					
2	xx/xx/19xx	10	Cash	✓	xxx	00		
		20	Accounts Receivable				xxx	00
		70	Sales				xxx	00
			To record daily cash sales and payments from house accounts					
3	xx/xx/19xx	80	Cost of Goods Sold	✓	xxxx	00		
		30	Inventory				xxxx	00
			To record dail cost of sales					
4	xx/xx/19xx	70	Sales		xx	00		
		10	Cash				xx	00
			To correct posting error because of Grandpa Otis's penmanship					
		80	Inventory		xx	00		
		10	Cash				xx	00
			To recored cash refund and return of merchandise purchased previous month					
		75	Sales Returns & Allowances		xx	00		
		80	Cost of Goods Sold				xx	00
			To record reversal of previous month sale					
5	xx/xx/19xx	70	Sales		x	00		
		20	Accounts Receivable				x	00
			To record merchandise returned from previous days sale on account					

JOURNAL ENTRIES PREPARED BY GRANDMA OTIS. THESE JOURNAL ENTRIES ARE THE SUMMARY OF THE DAY'S TRANSACTIONS TO BE RECORDED TO THE GENERAL LEDGER ACCOUNTS.

The bookkeeper traditionally also pays the bills and does the payroll. Grandma Otis reviews all of the delivery receipts for the day and compares them to Grandpa Otis' merchandise bought book. Any items purchased for resale are summarized and recorded to the inventory general ledger account as a debit. The credit will be recorded to the accounts payable general ledger and to the vendor ledger if the vendor bill will be paid next month or to cash if paid out of the register or if a check was written. Every time a vendor bill comes in, Grandma Otis must take great care to ensure that the bill has not been previously recorded or paid before writing the check. Monthly utility bills are recorded as a debit to the utility expense account and a credit to accounts payable, to be paid on the due date. As Grandma Otis is writing checks to pay the utility bills currently due from the previous month, she is posting to the vendor ledger, a debit to accounts payable, and a credit to cash in the general ledger. You should now question if Grandpa Otis is keeping his books as cash basis or accrual basis. If you were paying attention, you know that the books are kept on the accrual basis. If Grandpa Otis was operating on a cash basis, sales by customers and purchases from vendors on account would not be recorded until the cash was paid to the vendor or received from the customer.

Grandma Otis calculates payroll and writes the checks to pay employees. She is recording the payroll to each employee ledger, then summarizing total payroll and recording a credit to cash and a debit to the related payroll expense accounts. The total payroll expense accounts must equal the total of all employee ledgers; otherwise, payroll reports and payroll taxes will be incorrect. The IRS could assess significant penalties to the general store.

At the end of each month, Grandma Otis will prepare an unadjusted trial balance. The unadjusted trial balance ensures that all debits and credits are equal across all general ledger accounts; if they are not, Grandma Otis must go through the month's work to figure out what is missing or recorded incorrectly. When debits and credits balance, the unadjusted trial balance is in balance. Grandma Otis sends the unadjusted trial balance and general ledger to the accountant for the preparation of financial statements and any tax filings that may need to be done. When the accountant completes the financial statements and tax work, adjustments are posted to the general ledger and an adjusted trial balance is prepared and returned to the Otis's. Adjustments to the general ledger made by the accountant could include depreciation, income tax expense, and allowance for doubtful accounts. At the end of each year, adjustments to close out all income statement accounts are made by posting an offsetting debit or credit to zero the account. To ensure that the trial balance and balance sheet "balance or total zero," the offset is recorded to retained earnings as a profit or loss.

By now, if you are confused, ready to pound your head against the wall or run away screaming, my job is done. If not, please reread the previous paragraphs until you believe Grandpa and Grandma Otis have had enough customers, bills and payroll, financial statements, and adjusted trial balances. The accounting cycle continues until the general store closes forever.

Double-entry bookkeeping consists of repetitive tasks that follow specific rules. Every individual and company has similar record-keeping needs. This includes knowing how much cash is on hand, where the next cash is going to come from, and the current cash needs. Computerizing double-entry bookkeeping was a natural progression with the introduction of computers to the business world,[81] as evidenced by the adoption of Herman Hollerith's mechanical tabulator in 1903 by Marshall Field's department store for cost accounting. (Review the first section and see the beautifully illustrated timeline in the first section if you skipped it.)

The development of a few different technologies have allowed for the evolution of today's accounting systems, from QuickBooks to the enterprise resource planning (ERP) systems like Oracle or SAP. These technologies have made paper ledgers and journals obsolete. The bookkeeper is no longer called a bookkeeper and is now known as an accounting clerk or staff accountant. The most significant development was the database. In the 2nd and 3rd generation computers, programming was tightly coupled to object-oriented programing or loose coupling in the 4th generation computers.

Components of Manaul Bookkeeping	Technology that made bookkeeping automation possible
Ledger Sheets	Flat Files
Pencils	Keypunch Devices
Customer / Vendor / Payroll Ledgers	Relational Databases
Posting	Interfaces
Sales Journals	Point of Sale & Bar Codes
Purchase Journals	

TECHNOLOGIES THAT HAVE MADE THE AUTOMATION OF BOOKKEEPING POSSIBLE

A person trained in double-entry bookkeeping rarely understands that the power of relational databases is simply to join two or more flat files with an index or that keypunch device technology evolved into the familiar keyboard or that bar code readers actually read the spaces between the bars. These are areas the technology professional should be well versed in. If your accountants start complaining that the transaction detail does not match with the customer accounts receivable, maybe the index is corrupt and rebuilding the databases is needed. If the inventory is showing excessive losses, maybe the bar codes are smudged and not reading correctly. If your accountants have a new dual monitor setup and they are complaining that the keyboard is not working, maybe they are looking at the wrong monitor — I myself am guilty of this!

Now that you have a basic understanding of how double-entry bookkeeping works, we can all agree that automation of these tasks was a good thing. Automated accounting systems have allowed companies to grow into the global entities we now take for granted. Imagine a Fortune 500 company with stacks of ledgers and pencils, or if Grandma Otis had more than a handful of house accounts. Well-designed and well-implemented automated accounting systems can provide a company's financial position at a moment's notice, which is number 3 on the Pacioli list of what every merchant needs to be successful (Chapter 3 if you skipped it).

As with every good thing, the bad comes with it. Today's vocational training for entry-level accounting staff looks more like data entry and navigation of today's most popular accounting packages, rather than the nuts and bolts of double-entry bookkeeping. Automation of the bookkeeping process has increased the complexity of the chart of accounts. In a poorly implemented and managed accounting system, tracking of complex transactions such as departmental expenses is done by adding another account to the general ledger rather than leveraging the power of relational databases. A well-designed, yet poorly implemented accounting package is the worst nightmare for both IT and the Accounting department. Manual work around procedures are often implemented rather than expending the resources to correct the accounting application. With the globalization of companies, accounting rules are becoming extremely complex. Automated accounting systems have put the Information Technology professional in a position where awareness of double-entry bookkeeping and the existence of accounting standards is necessary to ensure that the accounting application is properly processing transactions.

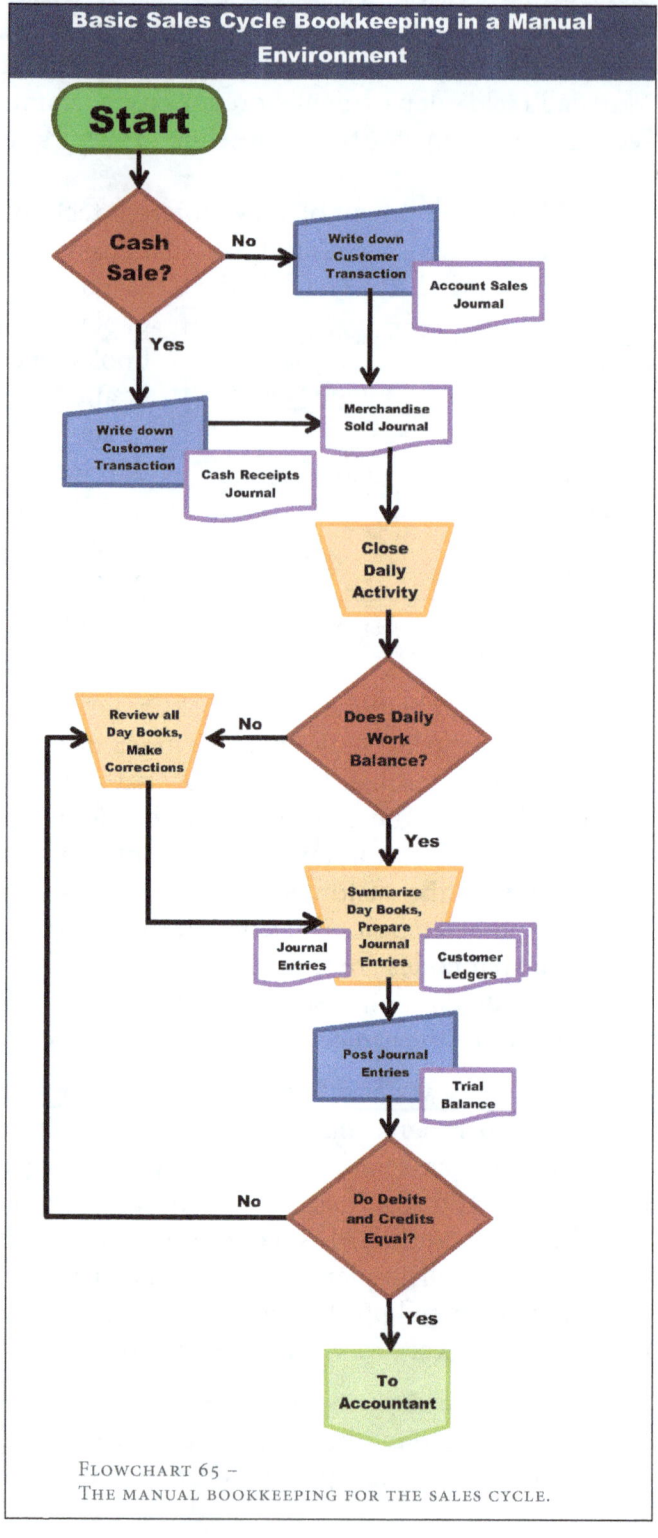

FLOWCHART 65 –
THE MANUAL BOOKKEEPING FOR THE SALES CYCLE.

A young accountant spends a week at his new office with the retiring accountant he is replacing. Each morning, as the more experienced accountant begins the day, he opens his desk drawer, takes out a worn envelope, removes a yellowing sheet of paper, reads it, nods his head, looks around the room with renewed vigor, returns the envelope to the drawer, and then begins his day's work. After he retires, the new accountant can hardly wait to read for himself the message contained in the envelope. Surely, he thinks to himself, it must contain the great secret to his mentor's success, a wondrous treasure of inspiration and motivation. His fingers tremble anxiously as he removes the mysterious envelope from the drawer and reads the following message: "Debits in the column on the left; Credits in the column on the right."[82]

CHAPTER 9

- FRIGGIN' BEAN COUNTERS -
WHAT DID YOU DO TO OUR COMPUTERS?

A guy in a bar leans over to the man next to him and says, 'Want to hear an accountant joke?' The man replies, 'Well, before you tell that joke, you should know that I'm 6 foot tall, 200 pounds, and I'm an accountant. And the guy sitting next to me is 6 foot 2 inches tall, 225 pounds, and he's an accountant too. Now, do you still want to tell that joke?' The first guy says, 'God no. Not if I'll have to explain it twice[83].'

Revenue Radicals or the Revenue Riot

Now that the fundamental concepts of double-entry bookkeeping have been resurrected, it is time to discuss the bookkeeping process in the automated accounting package. All of the concepts that apply to the manual bookkeeping system discussed in the preceding chapter apply to the automated accounting system.

Grandpa and Grandma Otis have long passed. Unfortunately, their waning days were spent in jail, because they decided not to pay income taxes on some of the sales from the general store. They used a high-tech invention called Liquid Paper to change the accounts receivable, sales, and cash numbers on the trial balance. As long as debits equaled credits and the trial balance was in balance, no one would notice, right? It did not take the tax man long to figure it out. What Grandpa and Grandma Otis forgot was the fact that the total of the individual customer ledgers must equal the accounts receivable general ledger and that the cash general ledger account must reconcile with the bank.

The Otis's great grandson, Sonny, has inherited the family business, but decided to rebrand the general store to repair the reputation of the family name. The big-box stores have moved into Small Town, USA, so Sonny Otis decided to become an office supply store called the Paper Clip Warehouse.

Sonny envisions a global business in the office supply market and is trying to decide the best way to track sales and do the accounting. To make an informed decision, he has asked the advice of his trusted accountant, and to ensure that the best decision is made, Sonny includes his IT professional in the discussion. As the Paper Clip Warehouse prepares for operations, Sonny is going to learn that the line between bookkeeping and accounting has become virtually unrecognizable and the days of playing at Grandma's feet while she posts journal entries are long gone.

Understanding Revenue

Companies exist for the sole purpose of making a profit for the owners. Profit is defined as the excess of revenue over expenses. Revenue is the primary means of achieving the goal of profits and can be referred to as top-line revenue, gross revenue, sales, or income. Simply defined, revenue means gross amounts generated from normal operating activities in terms of a monetary unit, such as dollars - $, sterling pounds - £, euros - €, etc. Net revenue or net sales is gross revenue or gross sales minus sales returns or discounts.

Unfortunately, revenue has become a term that is thrown about without clear meaning. Many times, revenue is used erroneously as a synonym for profit. The CEO might say in the strategic planning meetings, "We must increase our top-line revenue because revenue is the reason we are in business." As we said, a business exists for the sole purpose of profit for the owners. Or the salesperson might say, "I have a big order from our sister company that is going to increase revenue for the company." We'll explain why this one is just plain wrong.

Revenue is derived from normal business operations. For example, if an organization is in the business of selling office supplies, then each sale of office supplies would be revenue at the point of sale. The sale of the shelves that display the office supplies or withdrawal of office supplies from inventory for use in the back office would not be revenue. Office supplies sold to a sister company could be recorded as revenue for the division that sold them and an expense for the division that consumed them; however, when the public financial statements are issued, the transaction will be treated as if it never occurred.

GAAP Rules for Proper Revenue Recognition[84]

GAAP has rules for the recording of revenue. Many industries have warranted special GAAP rules for revenue recognition. Such industries include software development, construction, and mining, to name a few. For most companies, revenue is recorded when a transaction occurring from ordinary business activities creates a claim to cash. A claim to cash means that revenue is realized or realizable. When revenue is recorded in the general ledger, it is said to be recognized. In accounting nerd speak, this is referred to as the culmination of earnings process, which simply means that revenue is recognized at the point of sale or when the service has been provided and a reasonable method for estimating collection of amounts owed to the company must exist. The GAAP revenue recognition that apply to the majority of business are:

- There is pervasive evidence that an arrangement exists - An arrangement occurs when there are 2 willing participants to a transaction. The transaction could be evidenced by a written contract or be as simple as paying for merchandise at the cash register.

- Delivery of the merchandise or performance of the service has occurred - The Company has fulfilled substantially all of its obligations related to the transaction. Substantially is a key word — how would your company define substantial fulfillment of their obligations?

- The selling price is fixed and determinable - The selling price or fee for services is known or is easily calculated by all parties to the transaction. For example, there is a contract for cleaning offices at $100 per office. If 10 offices are cleaned, revenue is $1,000.

- Collection is reasonably assured - The Company is confident that the customer will pay.

The revenue recognition rules appear simple, but when you consider all of the decision points, this is what you get: (See process flow on next page).

Sonny Otis has successfully collaborated with his IT professional and accountant, resulting in the purchase of a large commercially recognized ERP system. The ERP has been well planned and well implemented. It satisfies current needs and allows for the growth Sonny is planning. The ERP is set up to record transactions for the current and planned future expansion of the Paper Clip Warehouse.

Divisions	
100	Corporate Office
200	East Coast Sales
300	West Coast Sales
400	World-wide web sales
500	Distribution Center
600	Manufacturing Center
700	International Operations

CURRENT AND FUTURE PAPER CLIP WAREHOUSE DIVISIONS. THIS REPRESENTS A COMPLETE LISTING, EVEN THOUGH NOT ALL DIVISIONS ARE YET OPERATIONAL.

While each division within the company may have the following departments, our examples are going to be limited to departments 10 and 20; generally divisions and department identifiers are incorporated into the account code and used as an index for database reporting.

The chart of accounts has been expertly set up to capture all of the transactions and to produce meaningful financial information. A well designed and defined chart of accounts is one of the most important elements in setting up an automated accounting system. The chart of accounts should

Departments	
10	Administrative
20	Sales
30	Warehouse
40	Manufacturing

DEPARTMENTS WITHIN THE PAPER CLIP WAREHOUSE DIVISIONS. DEPARTMENTS OR COST CENTERS ARE SET UP IN THE ACCOUNTING APPLICATION WHEN MANAGEMENT WANTS REPORTING FOR COSTS BY DEPARTMENT

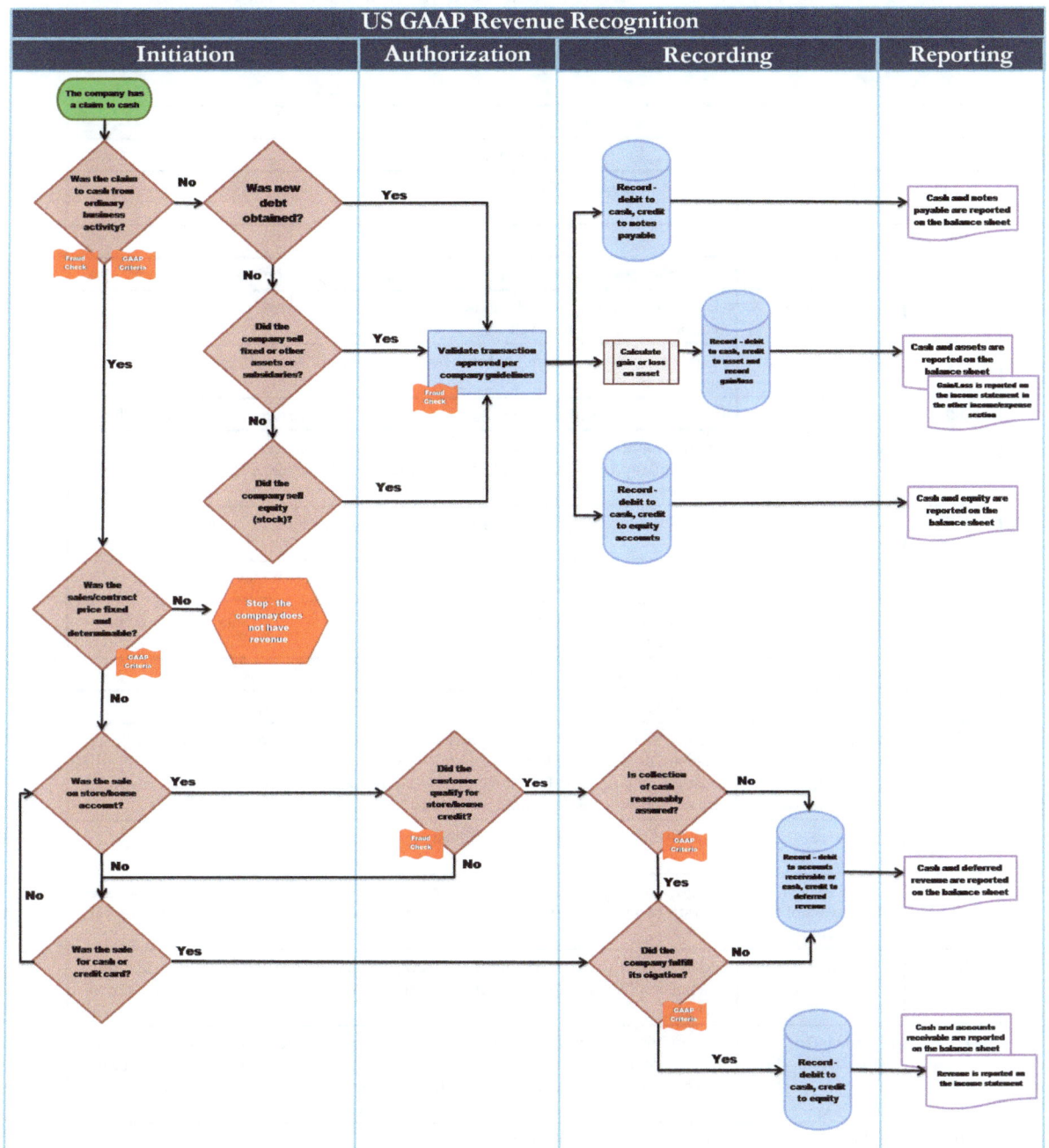

ACCOUNTING FOR REVENUE UNDER U.S. GAAP. THERE ARE MANY COMPLEX DECISION POINTS INVOLVED WHEN DETERMINING WHETHER REVENUE IS REALIZED OR REALIZABLE.

look very similar to a data dictionary. According to IBM, a data dictionary is a "centralized repository of information about data such as meaning, relationships to other data, origin, usage, and format."[85]

Paper Clip Warehouse Office Supplies		
Chart of Accounts		
Account Code	Account Title	Account Purpose and Definition
Balance Sheet Accounts		
10000	Assets	Economic resources that represent ownership and can be converted to cash
11000	Current Assets	Cash and other assets that are either converted to cash or consumed the longer of a year or in the operating cycle
11100	Cash - Operating	Money generated as a result of business operations, each operating unit will have a cash account
11200	Cash - Investing	Excess cash that is invested in short-term marketable securities per company policy
11300	Petty Cash	Small amounts of currency maintained at the operating level to ensure that operations are not disrupted; could include cash for change and a small fund for miscellaneous expenses
11400	Accounts Receivable	Debts owed by customers for services rendered or merchandise delivered
11410	Allowance for Doubtful Accounts	Account that records the portion of accounts receivable that may not be collected. The allowance for doubtful accounts is only an estimate The purpose is to ensure that the conservatism convention is adhered to and the accounts receivable is stated at the net realizable value
11420	Deposits	Cash paid to insure future performance or security
11430	Prepaid Expense	Annual payments for insurance premiums, business, and software license fees
11500	Inventory	The raw materials and work-in-process for goods manufactured for resale and the finished goods that are held for resale Inventory is one of the most important assets that most businesses have. Inventory turnover represents the primary sources of revenue and earnings for the shareholders/owners
11600	Long Term Investments	Investments that are held for more than a year
12000	Fixed Assets or Property Plant & Equipment (PPE)	Long-term tangible property that is owned and used by the company for business operations and is not expected to be consumed or converted into cash within the year
12100	Furniture, Fixtures & Equipment (FFE)	Movable furniture, fixtures, or other equipment that are not permanently connected to a building. These items are necessary for the business operations and the production of revenue
12110	Accumulated Depreciation - FFE	The cumulative depreciation of an asset up to a single point in its life. The depreciation during a single period is added to the previous period's accumulated depreciation to get the current accumulated depreciation. The purpose is to ensure that the conservatism convention and matching principle are adhered to.
12200	Building	Physical structures permanently attached to land
12210	Accumulated Depreciation – Building	The cumulative depreciation of an asset up to a single point in its life. The depreciation during a single period is added to the previous period's accumulated depreciation to get the current accumulated depreciation. The purpose is to ensure that the conservatism convention and matching principle are adhered to.
12300	Land	Portions of the earth's surface that are owned by the company

\multicolumn{3}{c}{Paper Clip Warehouse Office Supplies}
\multicolumn{3}{c}{Chart of Accounts}
Account Code	Account Title	Account Purpose and Definition
12400	Land Improvements	Land improvements such as parking lots and landscaping
12410	Accumulated Depreciation - Land Improvements	The cumulative depreciation of an asset up to a single point in its life. The depreciation during a single period is added to the previous period's accumulated depreciation to get the current accumulated depreciation. The purpose is to ensure that the conservatism convention and matching principle are adhered to.
20000	Liabilities	Obligations from past transactions or events. Settlement will result in the transfer or use of assets or other future economic benefit
21000	Accounts Payable	Obligations from past transactions or events that have occurred for the business operations
21100	Trade Payable	Obligations due to vendors for supplies used in the generation of revenue
21200	Salaries/Wages Payable	Obligations due to employees working for the generation of revenue
21300	Taxes payable	Obligations due to taxing authorities
22000	Deferred Revenue	Advance payments recorded on the balance sheet as a liability, until the services have been rendered or products have been delivered. Deferred revenue is a liability. It is revenue that has not been earned because the products or services are owed to the customer.
23000	Current Portion of Notes Payable	Portion of long-term note payables that are due within 12 months
24000	Interest Payable	Interest due on notes payable
25000	Notes Payable	Long-term loans that are owed
26000	Contingent Liabilities	Potential future obligations that are based on current events Contingent liabilities are recorded only if the future obligation is probable and the amount of the liability can be estimated
27000	Due to / Due from	Account for recording transactions between related companies, such as divisions within a single entity
30000	Stockholders Equity or Owners Equity	Capital (money) contributions from investors/owners in exchange for stock or ownership shares. Stockholders' / Owners' equity represents the ownership stake on the books by investors and owners
31000	Common Stock	Representation of a share of ownership in a company that issues stock stated at face value (par value)
32000	Additional Paid in Capital	Money paid over the par value of the stock
33000	Retained Earnings	Accumulation of the profits and losses over the life of the company
	Current Year Net Income/(Loss)	
Income Statement Accounts		
40000	Revenue	Gross income that a company receives from normal business activities
41000	Sales	Transactions in which buyers of the company's products receive tangible or intangible products or services, generally in exchange for money.
41100	Sales Discounts	Used to track coupons and other promotions
41110	Sales Returns & Allowances	Used to track merchandise returns

	Paper Clip Warehouse Office Supplies	
	Chart of Accounts	
Account Code	Account Title	Account Purpose and Definition
50000	Cost of Sales (COGS)	Direct costs for the production or acquisition of goods sold by a company
51000	Purchases	Acquisition of goods for sale
52000	Freight In	Freight costs for acquiring goods for sale
60000	Expenses	All costs (obligations), other than COGS, that are incurred through operations to earn revenue
61000	Salaries	Payroll dollars paid to salaried employees
61100	Wages	Payroll dollars paid to hourly employees
61200	Freight Out	Costs incurred with shipping products to customers
61300	Rent	Costs incurred for the use of property or equipment
61400	Utilities	Costs incurred for public utilities, such as electric, water/sewer, trash
61500	Telephone	Costs incurred with the telephone service and/or system
61600	Advertising	Costs incurred to get the word out regarding the products and services offered
61700	Repairs and Maintenance	Costs incurred for repairs and maintenance of PPE
61800	Office Supplies	Costs incurred for administrative supplies
61900	Contract Labor	Costs incurred for temporary labor
62000	Insurance	Costs incurred for insurance
63000	Staffing Fees	Costs incurred for training and recruitment
64000	Licenses Fees	Costs incurred for software license fees
65000	Bad Debt Expense	Accounts receivable that is not collectible
67000	Depreciation Expense	The systematic recognition of expenses associated with the use of Fixed Assets in the generation of revenue
67100	Interest Expense	Cost incurred for interest on debt
67200	Tax Expense	Taxes incurred
67300	Gain/Loss on sale of assets	Asset sales where the costs - depreciation results in a gain or a loss
67400	Interest Income	Interest earned from investments
67500	Unrealized Gain/Loss on Investments	Unrealized gains and losses from investments

PAPER CLIP WAREHOUSE CHART OF ACCOUNTS. A CHART OF ACCOUNTS DEFINES HOW A COMPANY WILL RECORD TRANSACTIONS TO THE GENERAL LEDGER AND SERVICES AS THE DATABASE KEY OR INDEX.

The Paper Clip Warehouse began setting up operations December 1, 20xx, and opened for business on December 29, 20xx. The first step in setting up a business is to secure operating capital. Operating capital is the cash needed to pay for day-to-day operations. There are only three ways a business can obtain cash: ordinary business operations, taking on debt, or contributions from the owners.

On December 1, 20xx, the Paper Clip Warehouse completed the following transactions:

1. A note payable was signed for $10,000,000, payable in 60 monthly installments at 3% annual interest.
2. 10,000 shares of common stock with $10 par value for $40 per share were sold.

These transactions are examples of new debt and obtaining money from the owners.

Journal entries are prepared using end-user computing applications, such as a recognized spreadsheet application. All supporting documentation is attached to the journal entry and submitted to the CFO for review and approval prior to posting. Since these transactions do not affect any subsidiary ledger, they are uploaded to the general ledger.

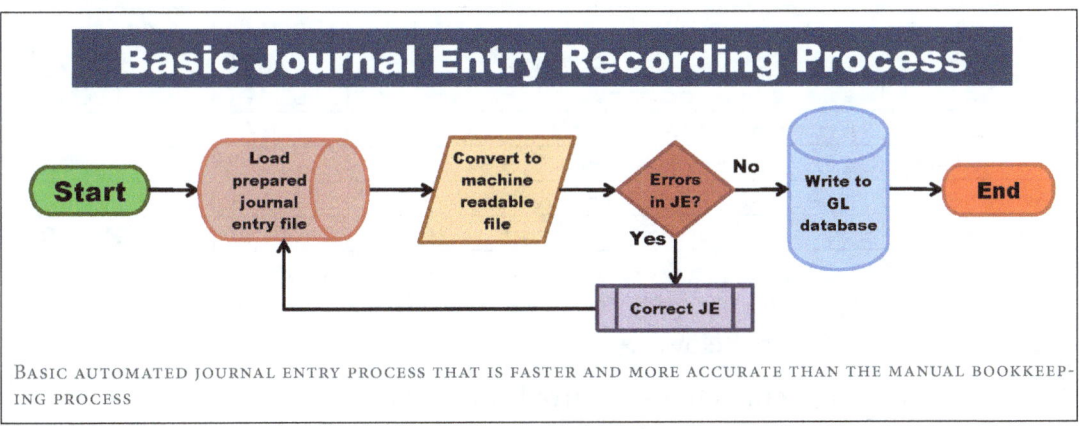

BASIC AUTOMATED JOURNAL ENTRY PROCESS THAT IS FASTER AND MORE ACCURATE THAN THE MANUAL BOOKKEEPING PROCESS

Transaction Date	Ref Num	Account			Account Title	Debit	Credit
		account code	division	department			
Dec. 1, 20xx	1	11100	100	10	Cash - Operating	$ 10,000,000.00	
		23000	100	10	Current Portion of Notes Payable		$ 833,333.33
		25000	100	10	Notes Payable		$ 9,166,666.67
		To record the 60 month, 3% note payable for setting up business					
	2	11100	100	10	Cash - Operating	$ 4,000,000.00	
		31000	100	10	Common Stock		$ 100,000.00
		32000	100	10	Additional Paid in Capital		$ 3,900,000.00
		To record 10,000 shares of common stock, $10 par value for $40 per share.					

JOURNAL ENTRY PREPARED BY THE ACCOUNTING CLERK FOR UPLOAD TO THE ERP. DESPITE THE ADVANCES IN ACCOUNTING APPLICATIONS, CARE MUST STILL BE TAKEN IN PREPARING INPUTS TO THE SYSTEM!

Error checking is a critical task in the automated accounting system. Just like the manual bookkeeping system, the debits must equal credits and the ERP has built-in function to validate this. In addition, the error-checking routine will validate the account numbers and ensure that all required information (essential elements) is included in the journal entry.

The transactions in this example are not part of the normal business operations; therefore no revenue is recognized. These transactions are going to affect the assets, liabilities, and equity accounts of the balance sheet. Remember, balance sheet accounts are real accounts that include cash and any account that has a cash value either owed to or owed by the business.

After much preparation, the Paper Clip Warehouse is ready to open its doors for business on December 29. A state of the art point-of-sale (POS) system has been implemented. The system is set up to perform a nightly batch processing of sales and interface the results to the accounting system. Standard transaction

POS Transaction Codes			
Code	Description	General Ledger Account Mapping	
		Debit	Credit
Cash	Cash/Credit Card Sale	11100	41000
On_Acct	Sale on Account	11400	41000
Pay_Acct	Payment on Account	11100	11400
Cash_Ret	Cash Sales Return	41110	11100
Acct_Ret	On Account Sales Return	41110	11400
Deposit	Special Order Deposit	11100	22000

STANDARD POS TRANSACTIONS CODES MAPPED TO THE DEBIT AND CREDIT GENERAL LEDGER ACCOUNTS. THESE CODES ARE BEING LEVERAGED BY PAPER CLIP WAREHOUSE AS IT COMMENCES OPERATIONS.

codes used in the POS are below.

The following transactions occurred at the POS:

3. December 29 – Cash and credit card sales: East Coast Division $1,100; West Coast Division $3,640.

4. December 29 – Sales on account: East Coast customer Don Magnet $42,892; West Coast customer Rick Entertainer $9,624

5. December 30 – West Coast sales sold $1,500 worth of inventory to the corporate office.

6. December 30 – East Coast store accepted a special custom order for office furniture from Don Magnet for $100,000. The terms of the sale were 1/2 down with the remainder due 30 days after full delivery.

7. December 31 – 1/4 of Don Magnet's order was obtained through a third-party. The delivery service was called and the order was placed in the designated pick-up area of the loading dock for shipment FOB-shipping point.

All transactions in examples 3—7 above are considered the Paper Clip Warehouse's ordinary course of business, which is selling office supplies for a fixed price. When collection is reasonably assured, we can recognize revenue. At the point of sale, cash and collection of credit card charges are reasonably assured, and customers with Paper Clip Warehouse house accounts have been screened and have good credit histories.

The nightly batch processing begins with an error check that is going to ensure that each transaction code from the POS system has an account mapping to the accounting system, the POS system was properly closed out, and the transactions are complete. Batch processing will also check that the customer accounts are valid. The individual customer transactions will be written to the customer ledger. Remember that the total of the ending balance of all customer ledgers must equal the general ledger accounts receivable account. The basic functionality of the nightly batch processing and the journal entries for transactions 3—6 are below.

Transaction 5, the West Coast sale of $1,500 worth of inventory to the corporate office, is going to post to the Error Reject Queue because it was entered in the POS system as a miscellaneous customer. The miscellaneous customer account was not set up in the accounting system, and the corporate office was not set up as a customer in

Transaction Date	Ref Num	Account			Account Title	Debit	Credit
		account code	division	department			
Dec. 29, 20xx	3	11100	200	20	Cash - Operating	$ 1,100.00	
		41000	200	20	Sales		$ 1,100.00
		11100	300	20	Cash - Operating	$ 3,640.00	
		41000	300	20	Sales		$ 3,640.00
					To record daily cash and credit card sales		
	4	11400	200	20	Accounts Receivable	$ 42,892.00	
		41000	200	20	Sales		$ 42,892.00
		11400	300	20	Accounts Receivable	$ 9,624.00	
		41000	300	20	Sales		$ 9,624.00
					To record daily sales on account		
Dec. 30, 20xx	5	27000	300	20	Due to/Due from	$ 1,500.00	
		41000	300	20	Sales		$ 1,500.00
					To record sale of office supplies to corporate office		
	6	11100	200	20	Cash - Operating	$ 50,000.00	
		11400	200	20	Accounts Receivable	$ 50,000.00	
		41000	200	20	Deferred Revenue		$ 100,000.00
					To record daily sales on account		

JOURNAL ENTRIES FOR TRANSACTIONS 3-6 ABOVE. AS ILLUSTRATED, THE SALES AND DEFERRED REVENUE

the POS. The correct accounting treatment for this transaction is as an inter-company transaction. To repeat: to record revenue, there must be 2 willing participants to a transaction. While West Coast sales and the corporate office are 2 willing participants, they share common ownership. From an accounting standpoint, they are considered one entity. The economic reality of the transaction is the same as taking money out of one pocket and putting it into another (do you have more money?), or moving the laptop from the bedroom to the den (do you now have 2 laptops?). It is permissible to show the revenue for $1,500 recorded to West Coast sales and the expense recorded to the corporate office for internal-segment operating statements. When the financial statements are prepared for public scrutiny, the transaction will be eliminated after all of the segment general ledger accounts are added together.

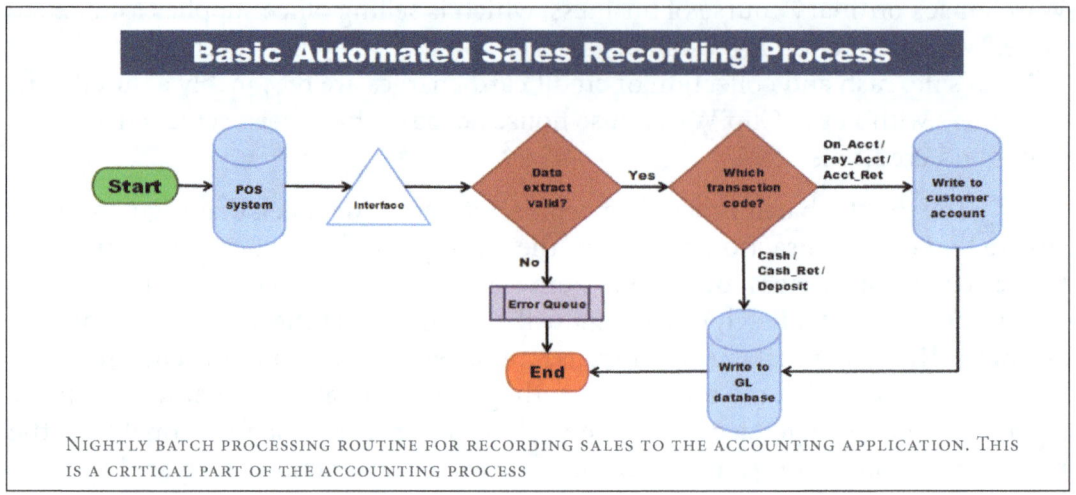

Nightly batch processing routine for recording sales to the accounting application. This is a critical part of the accounting process

Transaction 6 will post as a normal sale because the transaction codes Cash and On_Acct are mapped to credit revenue in the general ledger and the customer has a valid accounts receivable established. We know that the system posting of this transaction is going to be incorrect. The customer made a special order that has not been delivered. Therefore, no revenue can be recorded because the company has not substantially completed its obligation. This is an example of a transaction from the ordinary course of business that cannot be recognized as revenue. However, the transaction occurred, so an entry has to be made. When the company accepted the order and took the cash deposit, they accepted an obligation to perform.

Each morning, the accounting staff will review and validate the posting through the nightly interface to the general ledger. These two transactions will need to be corrected with journal entries.

On December 31, 20xx, the Warehouse notified accounting that 1/4 of Don Magnet's order was ready for delivery. The delivery service was called and the order was placed on the loading dock for shipment free on board (FOB-shipping point). The accounting for orders that are to be delivered at a future time causes problems from an accounting perspective. "FOB shipping point" and "FOB origin" further add confusion to revenue recognition. These shipping methods must be considered in order to determine whether the company has substantially fulfilled its obligation. "FOB shipping point" states that the buyer will pay shipping costs and take responsibility for the goods when they leave the seller's premises. "FOB destination" means the seller will pay shipping costs and remain responsible for the goods until the buyer takes possession. In addition, how does Accounting know that the merchandise delivered actually represents 1/4 of Don Magnet's order, the delivery service was actually called with a pick-up order, and the order is sitting in the designated area of the loading dock? Is there a stipulation in the sales order that requires the entire order be delivered at one time? What assurance is there that the items obtained from the third party are of the same quality that the Paper Clip Warehouse would deliver and that the items conform to the customer's specification? If any one of these questions cannot be answered affirmatively, then the company has not substantially fulfilled 1/4 of its obligation and revenue cannot be recognized. For now, the assumption is that all of these questions pass the test and the journal entry to record the transaction is below.

			Journal Entry			
Transaction Date	Ref Num	Account			Debit	Credit
		account code	division	department	Account Title		
Dec. 31, 20xx	7	22000	200	20	Deferred Revenue	$ 25,000.00	
		41000	200	20	Sales		$ 25,000.00
		To record revenue from delivery of 1/4 of Don Magnet's order					

THE JOURNAL ENTRY FOR TRANSACTION 7. IN THIS JOURNAL ENTRY, 1/4TH OF THE PURCHASE BY DON MAGNET CAN BE RECORDED AS REVENUE BECAUSE THE PAPER CLIP WAREHOUSE SUBSTANTIALLY FULFILLED 1/4TH OF ITS OBLIGATION

IFRS & Revenue Recognition

Businesses are fluid entities, and as new markets are developed, new and unique transactions are executed. We previously mentioned International Financial Reporting Standards (IFRS) in Chapter 3 as the accounting standard that is being adopted by many countries around the world. Prior to the 1990s, most countries had their own accounting standards; they were all based on different conceptual frameworks. By the end of the 20th century, two predominant standards prevailed: the U.S. GAAP and the IFRS.

U.S. GAAP is a rule-based approach, and IFRS is a principles-based approach to accounting. The primary difference in these accounting standards is the methodology used to assess the accounting treatment of transactions. The rule-based approach is just that: a system of rules that have been accepted as standard practices wherein similar transactions receive the same accounting treatment. The principles-based approach has the potential for different accounting treatments for similar transactions.

The International Accounting Standards Board (IASB) and the Financial Accounting Standards Board (FASB) began a convergence project intended to move to one global set of accounting standards. The first joint project toward convergence undertaken by the FASB and IASB began in 2002 for revenue recognition; the final standard is expected to be released in 2014. All companies that currently prepare financial statements in accordance with either U.S. GAAP or IFRS are currently required to adopt the standard by 2017. Revenue is one of the most important numbers to the users of financial statements, because revenue is the first step to profit and a business exists to make a profit for the owners. Under current U.S. GAAP, revenue recognition concepts are defined but are subject to a significant amount of interpretation by management. There are over 200 specialized or industry-specific requirements for revenue recognition. IFRS has fewer requirements, but they are vague, difficult to understand, and difficult to apply. It has taken 12-plus years for the two primary accounting standard setters to agree, despite some very similar concepts. The similarities in revenue recognition between both sets of standards include:

- Both IFRS and U.S. GAAP tie revenue recognition to the completion of the earnings process, point of sale, or services rendered, and the realization of an asset, such as cash.
- Revenue will result from the business's ongoing operations and represent expected cash inflows.
- Revenue is not recognized until it is realized or realizable, claim to cash and earned, signifying the earnings process is completed.
- Revenue is recognized when the buyer has accepted the goods or services.

Given the 12-plus years it took to get to this point, does that leave any new standards unlikely to happen? Make no mistake; accounting standards are a politically charged endeavor. This is an area to monitor with great interest.

Contractual arrangements define the criteria for each party's responsibility for a transaction. An executed written contract determines when a company can recognize revenue. IFRS and U.S. GAAP have a slight difference when discussing contractual arrangements: IFRS defines the recognition criteria as measured reliably, and U.S. GAAP defines it as a fixed and determinable price or consideration (amount paid by customer).

One difference between U.S. GAAP and IFRS related to rules-based versus principles-based methodologies is that IFRS requires a significant amount of disclosure. Under IFRS, if one accounting treatment for a transaction is selected over another, the company is required to fully disclose the rationale for selecting the accounting treatment. These types of nuances could have a significant impact on information technology supporting the business process as well as accounting as the U.S. aligns with the rest of the world through IFRS and U.S. GAAP convergence. For example, it may become necessary to include unrestricted text fields for notes or capturing new data points. Depending on the impact convergence has on your company, new system implementations or modifications to and reconfigurations of existing systems may become necessary.

Expense Extremist - Understanding Expenses

The Paper Clip Warehouse would not be able to conduct business without purchasing store, office, and warehouse space, furniture and fixtures; inventory, and hiring staff. The company will also have to purchase insurance, utilities, advertising, and repairs and maintenance, and pay various taxes, just to name a few expenses. GAAP has specific rules for the recording of expenses. Expenses are classified in three ways: directly associated with earning revenue, benefitting future periods, and/or immediately benefitting the business. Expenses associated with the main revenue-generating activity of a business are called operating expenses. All other expenses are considered non-operating. Purchases recorded to a general ledger expense account that affects the income statement (nominal account) means that the expense has been recognized and incurred without regard to when it will be paid; in other words, the expense is benefiting the current accounting period. Purchases recorded to the general ledger balance sheet (real accounts) are assets or prepaid expenses, and are also known as capitalized expenses. For example, an annual insurance premium is going to benefit each month over a 12–month period. When the premium is paid, it is recorded to a prepaid asset account with a debit. At the end of each month, 1/12th of the premium will be recorded to an expense account on the income statement. The prepaid insurance account on the balance sheet is credited (decreased), while the expense on the income statement is debited (increased). Items purchased for resale at a later date are recorded as a debit to the general ledger balance sheet inventory account. As merchandise is sold, the balance sheet inventory account is credited and a debit is recorded to the income statement cost of goods sold account. Property, plant, and equipment are recorded as debits to the balance sheet and systematically recorded as expenses through the depreciation process.

The bookkeeping treatment for expenses is deceptively simple. Determining the appropriate accounting treatment for expenses can be tricky. It is possible for one expense to meet the criteria for each of the expense classifications. For example, the Paper Clip Warehouse purchases cash register receipt tape for resale to customers. This is the same receipt tape that fits the POS system the stores use. When a delivery of the receipt tape is accepted, the store shelves are stocked for resale to customers, the store supply closet is stocked for store use, and the remainder is stored in the warehouse for future shelf restocking. Depending on how a company has set up the accounting, this one purchase can debit the inventory and/or prepaid expense accounts on the balance sheet, and/or the cost of goods sold and/or supplies expense on the income statement. The best way to determine the proper accounting treatment for expenses is to understand the purpose of the initial purchase.

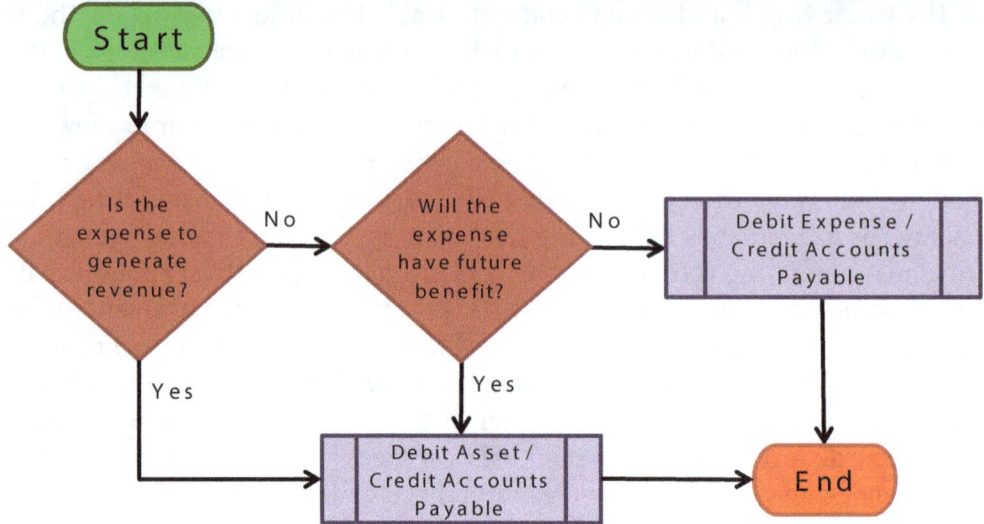

Accounting for expenses under U.S GAAP. It is driven by whether the expense is an operating expense and if not, when it will benefit the business.

The accounting systems and configurations used for managing the accounts payable function of an organization can be as unique as the organization itself. An accounts payable module within an ERP will have the following attributes: a purchasing approval procedure; a vendor setup and approval procedure; a vendor master file with all relevant vendor information, such as address, tax identification numbers, payment terms, and other information; and default general ledger account numbers. Remember that the total of all ending balances of the vendor ledgers must equal the ending accounts payable general ledger balance.

The default general ledger account numbers (also known as the primary key in the database) are used to automatically post any invoice that is input to the vendor ledger in the accounts payable module to the general ledger. Account posting can be set up as real-time or batch posting. In the case of Paper Clip Warehouse, that number is 21000. Then, each vendor record is set up with a typical (default) debit account number, usually an expense account on the income statement. The typical process flow for accounts payable may look like the diagram below.

The Paper Clip Warehouse made the following purchases in December to prepare for the store's opening and continuing operations. The evidence of purchase (invoice, contract, check request, employee expense reimbursement, etc.) is going to be input into the accounts payable module by the accounts payable clerk. All vendor ledger accounts are set up to credit the accounts payable general ledger

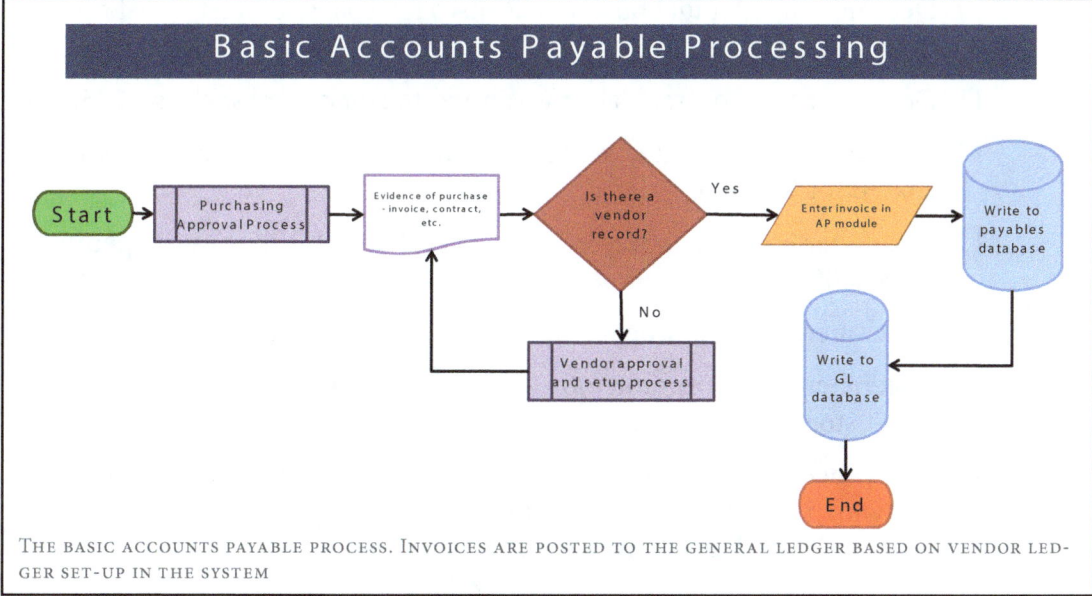

The basic accounts payable process. Invoices are posted to the general ledger based on vendor ledger set-up in the system.

control account; however, the debit side of the entry will be keyed in by the accounts payable clerk.

1. December 3 – Vacant land was purchased for a future expansion - $105,000.

2. December 4 – Two stores were purchased for cash: East Coast for $2,000,000 and West Coast for $5,000,000; corporate office space was leased for $14,000 per month, with first month's rent and security deposit of one month paid.

3. December 5 – Repairs were made on the East Coast parking lot for $50,000 and the West Coast sprinkler system for $14,000.

4. December 5 – Furniture and fixtures were purchased - East Coast $20,000, West Coast $45,000, and corporate office $10,000.

5. December 6 – Computers and network equipment were purchased for the Paper Clip Warehouse POS and wide are network (WAN) set up for $200,000.

6. December 6 – A national geek firm was retained to set up and install Paper Clip Warehouse WAN - $90,000.

7. December 6 – Recruitment fees for hiring staff at all locations - $90,000.

8. December 7 – Inventory was purchased - East Coast $40,000, West Coast $40,000, with shipping costs for each location of $2,000.

9. December 8 – Annual user licenses for the accounting and POS software were purchased - 50 at $1,000 per year.

10. December 8 – Annual business licenses for East and West Coast operations - $1,200 each.
11. December 8 – Contract labor was hired to stock store shelves - $25,000.
12. December 8 – Blanket coverage annual insurance policies were purchased for $24,000.
13. December 9 – Local advertising was purchased for the grand opening for $5,000.
14. December 10 – Training for newly hired staff - $6,000.
15. December 30 – Corporate office purchased supplies from West Coast store.
16. December 30 – 1/4 of Don Magnet's order was purchased from a third party for $10,000, with an additional $50 for shipping. Shipping the order to Don Magnet cost $50.00.
17. December 31 – Staff were paid for the pay period ending December 24, 20xx. Corporate salaries for the 2–week period were $10,000, wages were $2,000. East Coast salaries were $5,000, wages were $1,000. West Coast salaries were $6,100, wages $1,200. Payroll tax expense is 20% of total salaries and wages. A large recognized payroll service is used that also pays and files any necessary payroll taxes.
18. December 31 – An invoice for a $5,000 firewall was received by accounts payable, purchased on December 14, 20xx.

The difference between a capitalized or prepaid expense, recorded on the balance sheet as an asset, and a period expense, recorded on the income statement as an expense item, is the expectation of future benefit. The future benefit or estimated useful life of an asset is an estimation of the number of accounting periods the asset is expected to provide benefit. The future benefit should be reevaluated when repairs to extend the life are necessary or the asset has to be replaced. There is a significant amount of guidance from both accounting standard setters and various taxing authorities on the subject of estimated useful lives.

The Paper Clip Warehouse raised a significant amount of capital to set up and fund operations. Sonny Otis decided to open one store on the East Coast and one on the West Coast, with corporate administrative offices close to the West Coast store.

Vacant land was purchased for future expansion. Accounts payable was provided with all the necessary paperwork, including the deed and a bill of sale for entry into the accounts payable system. Review of the vacant land deed confirms that the land is in fact vacant. The bill of sale is entered into the accounts payable module, and the offsetting debit entry goes to the land account number 12300, division 100, for the total purchase price of $105,000.

Store property purchased for the East and West Coast operations included in the land, parking lot, and building. Accounts payable was provided with the deeds, bills of sale, and appraisals that allocate the purchase price between the land, parking lot, and building. It is necessary to allocate the purchase price because of the different expected estimated useful lives of the assets. The calculation will affect both financial reporting and income tax calculations. Proper support and justification of the allocations is critical for audit, financial reporting support, and income tax support.

The dollars allocated to land are based on the fair market value of comparable acreage in the areas for vacant land. The allocations for the buildings and parking lots are also based on comparable fair market values for the areas. The stores will be recorded to divisions 200 and 300 under department 10.

The accounts payable clerk was provided with a fully executed lease as support for the Corporate Office lease expense. The first month's rent and a deposit equal to one month's rent was required to take occupancy of the offices. The deposit is expected to benefit a future period, so the debit is going to be recorded to 11420-Deposits. The rent for the current month will be recorded to 61300-Rent

	GL Account #	% of purchase price	Purchase price allocation	
			East Coast	West Cost
Purchase Price	21000	100%	(2,000,000)	(5,000,000)
Land	12300	35%	700,000	1,750,000
Land Improveme	12400	15%	300,000	750,000
Building	12200	50%	1,000,000	2,500,000
Control Total			-	-

THE PURCHASE PRICE ALLOCATION FOR THE EAST COAST AND WEST COAST STORES. IT IS BEST TO OBTAIN THIS INFORMATION FROM EXPERTS.

Expense. Both will be to division 100 and department 10. The Accounts Payable clerk is setting up 11 recurring transactions of $14,000 to post rent expense and set up the payable to the landlord on the same day each month.

During the setup of the stores for opening day, it was noticed that the sprinkler system in the West Coast store leaked and the parking lot at the East Coast store had big potholes. Both of these issues were repaired. To determine the proper accounting treatment for repairs, you must consider the nature of the repairs. They can be ordinary recurring repairs, such as service contracts to periodically service the HVAC, or nonrecurring repairs, such as when the copy machine is broken and we cannot do any work until it is fixed.

Service contracts can warrant unique accounting treatments; the contract terms must be clearly understood. A service contract purchased and paid for on an annual basis will benefit more than one period. The payment for the service contract is recorded as a debit to the prepaid expense account on the balance sheet, and 1/12th of the amount is expensed monthly. A service contract can also be a fee for service, for example, when a service technician will come in on a periodic basis, perform the service, and leave a bill for the services rendered. These would be recorded as expenses when the services are performed. A service contract can also be a prepaid fee, initially recorded to prepaid expense (balance sheet). As services are rendered, an entry is made to credit prepaid expense and debit the appropriate expense (income statement).

Non-contracted ordinary repairs keep assets in good operating condition or are performed as needed to repair the asset. These repairs benefit the current period, so they are expensed as incurred. Nonrecurring repairs could be a repair to get the asset operational or a significant major overhaul. Significant major repairs are capitalized if the useful life of the asset is going to exceed the original estimates.

The repair to the sprinkler system was needed to keep the asset in good working order, so the $14,000 repair is expensed to 61700 - Repairs and Maintenance, division 300, department 10. The repair of the parking lot is going to restore the full recommended useful life, and the $50,000 repair is going to be added to 12400 - Land Improvements, division 200, department 10.

The purchase of furniture and fixtures is capitalized (recorded to the balance sheet as an asset), because it will benefit more than one period. The general ledger account is going to be 12100 – Furniture, Fixtures, and Equipment and the department will be 10, with $20,000 to division 200, $45,000 to division 300, and $10,000 to division 100.

The wide-area network (WAN) is being designed, built, and implemented by a national geek firm for $90,000. Computers and other network equipment were purchased for $300,000. While the purchase of the computers and network equipment are clearly going to benefit future periods, what about the $90,000 for the national geek firm? The rule is any expense incurred to prepare the asset for its intended use is capitalized as part of the cost of the asset. The capitalization for the network is going to be $390,000. This amount should be allocated among the divisions that are going to benefit from the network. Each division, East Coast, West Coast, and Corporate are going to benefit equally, so the entry is going to be $130,000 to account 12100 – Furniture, Fixtures and Equipment, divisions 100,

200, and 300, department 10 for each. Computer equipment could have a separate balance sheet account and usually does. The factors to consider when setting up the chart of accounts include the desire of management to separately track assets and liabilities, the significance of the expected capital investment, and/or regulatory reporting requirements.

Inventory of various office supplies was purchased for resale. Inventory is going to benefit more than one period; therefore, it will be posted to general ledger account 11500 - Inventory for divisions 200 and 300, department 20. Inventory includes the cost of obtaining or manufacturing an item for resale, plus any shipping and delivery charges.

Additional expenses incurred for the grand opening include staff recruitment and training, advertising, and contract labor. These expenses benefit the current period and will be posted to the income statement expense accounts. Allocation of an expense is a method to systematically divide a common expense among all areas of the business that benefit from the expense. Contract labor for stocking shelves and advertising is allocated at one-half to reflect the expense to the East and West Coast stores. Staff recruitment and training is allocated among the East and West Coast stores and the corporate office. An allocation can be done in any reasonable method that is meaningful to management. For expenses related to staffing, an allocation can be done based on the number of employees or it can be divided equally. The $96,000 paid for staff recruitment and training is going to be divided equally; $32,000 will be expensed to general ledger 63000 – Staffing Fees for divisions 100, 200, and 300, department 10. These fees can be further allocated to the departments based on the number of employees, depending on the level of detail management wants to see.

To round out the expenses needed for opening, three annual purchases were made for insurance, software license fees, and business licenses. These are going to affect more than one period, so they are all recorded to general ledger account 11430 - Prepaid Expenses, with the insurance and software license charged to division 100 and the business licenses charged to divisions 200 and 300.

During the opening, two purchasing transactions affecting sales occurred. The corporate office purchased supplies for the West Coast store, and 1/4 of Don Magnet's order was purchased from a third party. When the accounting clerks correct the rejected entry for transaction 5, an additional entry will be made to debit general ledger account 61800 - Office Supplies for division 100, department 10. The offset will be a credit to account 27000 - Due to/Due from for the $1,500. The purchase of Don Magnet's order is going to debit 51000 - Purchases for $10,000, 52000 - Freight In for $50, and 61200 - Freight Out for $50.

The next transaction posted to the general ledger is payroll. Payroll is processed by a well-recognized payroll company. The entry to record the transaction is posted by the staff accountants. The payroll company withdraws the entire payroll from the company cash account, so no liability exists for the Paper Clip Warehouse on payday.

The Accounting department begins preparing to close the books. The AP clerk receives an invoice for a firewall that was purchased during the month. The invoice does not indicate who ordered it or way it was ordered. The invoice for

Description	Account	Corporate	East Coast	West Coast
Salary	61000	10,000.00	5,000.00	6,100.00
Wages	61100	2,000.00	1,000.00	1,200.00
Taxes	61200	2,400.00	1,200.00	1,460.00
Cash	11100	(14,400.00)	(7,200.00)	(8,760.00)
		-	-	-

The payroll-related account entries. Because the payroll was drawn from cash, there is no liability for the Paper Clip Warehouse for this first payroll.

the firewall is going to be set aside until Accounts Payable can contact IT for more information. The best way to record expenses is to understand the initial intent. A firewall can be either hardware or software or both. As hardware, it has the potential to be capitalized as part of the network; as software, it could be capitalized as part of the network, or it could be treated as a separate intangible asset. Could this firewall be for a new program that management is implementing and therefore is a project cost and potentially a new asset? Should it be billed to a customer as a special order? Was it purchased as inventory for resale in the stores? The answer to each of these questions has a different accounting treatment that could cause large variances in operational results.

Unadjusted Trial Balance - Trial Balance on Trial

All of the known operational transactions affecting the period ending December 31, 20xx, have been recorded to the general ledger, except for the firewall, and an unadjusted trial balance is generated from the accounting system. After careful review of the trial balance, we can easily see that there are several missing transactions.

The missing transactions are utilities and telephone expenses, which should be accrued. Not receiving the bills does not supersede the requirement that all expenses incurred during the period must be recorded. Other missing expenses are recorded as part of the close process, such as depreciation and income tax expense.

At each period end closing, generating an unadjusted trial balance is the start of financial statement preparation. The accounting cycle is a term used to define the time a transaction occurs to the point it is included in the financial statements. Many accounting systems allow for continuation of the accounting

| | Paper Clip Warehouse - Unadjusted Trial Balance | | | |
| | December 31, 20xx | | | |
Account Code	Account Title	Corporate - 100	East Coast - 200	West Coast - 300
11100	Cash - Operating Corporate	13,985,600		
11105	Cash - Operating - East Coast		43,900	
11110	Cash - Operating - West Coast			(5,120)
11200	Cash - Investing			
11300	Petty Cash			
11400	Accounts Receivable		92,892	9,624
11410	Allowance for Doubtful Accounts			
11420	Deposits	14,000		
11430	Prepaid Expense	74,000	1,200	1,200
11500	Inventory		42,000	42,000
11600	Long Term Investments			
12100	Furniture, Fixtures & Equipment (FFE)	140,000	150,000	175,000
12110	Accumulated Depreciation - FFE			
12200	Building		1,000,000	2,500,000
12210	Accumulated Depreciation - Building			
12300	Land	105,000	700,000	1,750,000
12400	Land Improvements		350,000	750,000
12410	Accumulated Depreciation - Land Improvements			
21100	Trade Payable	(379,000)	(2,300,300)	(5,279,200)
21200	Salaries/Wages Payable			
21300	Taxes Payable			
21400	Accrued Liabilities			
22000	Deferred Revenue		(75,000)	
23000	Current Portion of Notes Payable	(833,333)		
24000	Interest Payable			
25000	Notes Payable	(9,166,667)		
26000	Contingent Liabilities			
27000	Due to/Due from	(1,500)		1,500
31000	Common Stock	(100,000)		
32000	Additional Paid in Capital	(3,900,000)		
33000	Retained Earnings			
41000	Sales		(68,992)	(14,764)
41100	Sales Discounts			
41110	Sales Returns & Allowances			
51000	Purchases		10,000	
52000	Freight In		50	
61000	Salaries	10,000	5,000	6,100
61100	Wages	2,000	1,000	1,200
61150	Payroll Tax Expense	2,400	1,200	1,460
61200	Freight Out		50	
61300	Rent	14,000		
61400	Utilities			
61500	Telephone			
61600	Advertising		2,500	2,500
61700	Repairs and Maintenance			14,000
61800	Office Supplies	1,500		
61900	Contract Labor		12,500	12,500
62000	Insurance			
63000	Staffing Fees	32,000	32,000	32,000
65000	Bad Debt Expense			
64000	Licenses Fees			
67000	Depreciation Expense			
67100	Interest Expense			
67200	Property Tax Expense			
67300	Gain/Loss on sale of assets			
67350	Income Tax Expense			
67400	Interest Income			
67500	Unrealized gain/loss on Investments			
	Check Figure	-	-	-

PAPER CLIP WAREHOUSE UNADJUSTED TRIAL BALANCE. THESE ARE THE ACCOUNT BALANCES DIRECTLY FROM THE GENERAL LEDGER. THE UNADJUSTED TRIAL BALANCE IS USED TO ENSURE DEBITS EQUAL CREDITS AND IS THE STARTING POINT FOR CLOSING ENTRIES.

cycle by supporting financial statement preparation. If you are still confused, it is okay – you are not accountants, and we are not done with the financial statement preparation. If you take away anything from the Paper Clip Warehouse, it is that our simple example got very complicated in a few areas.

Financial statement preparation can be done in either the accounting application, a third-party report writer that interfaces with the accounting application, or an end-user computing application. End-user computing applications have a significant risk associated with them, including formula errors and missing data. Regardless of how financial statements are prepared, it is important to be aware of the GAAP rules that must be followed for the preparation of financial statements that are going to be presented to the public.

What is the definition of "accountant"? Someone who solves a problem you didn't know you had in a way you don't understand.

CHAPTER 10

- FRIGGIN' BEAN COUNTERS -
WHAT'S IT MEAN? CLOSING THE GAP ON GAAP

To state the facts frankly is not to despair the future nor indict the past. The prudent heir takes careful inventory of his legacies and gives a faithful accounting to those whom he owes an obligation of trust.

~JOHN F. KENNEDY[88]

Paper Clip Warehouse Financials

The Paper Clip Warehouse has completed the year-end accounting close and is in the process of financial statement preparation for its first SEC filing. We know that the company is required to file financial statements in accordance with GAAP's assumption on reporting period. Typically, the SEC requires financial statements to be presented for three years, but since the Paper Clip Warehouse did not officially open for business until December 29, 20xx, the financial statements for the first year and the first month will be the same.

There are several entries that are missing from the unadjusted trial balance. The unadjusted trial balance is the start of financial statement preparation. The ending balance sheet balances need to be reconciled to ensure that each balance is supported and the financial statements are complete. Here is what we know so far and the GAAP assumptions, principles, or constraints that make including the following transactions necessary:

A. Materiality, Going Concern, and Historical Cost - A marketable securities account was opened on December 15, 20xx, for $5,000,000. $2,000,000 is intended as a long-term investment. Each store has a $1,200 bank to fund change for the POS system.

B. Matching - Management believes that 1.5% of the accounts receivable balance will not be collected.

C. Matching - Cost of goods sold must be recorded to match against the revenue. We know that the Paper Clip Warehouse marks up the inventory for sale by 40%.

D. Economic Entity - The intercompany sale of office supplies to the corporate office must be eliminated and recorded as withdrawal from inventory.

```
Cost of Goods Sold Calculation

Total Sales                          (83,756.00)
Less Sale to Corporate                 1,500.00
Less Don Magnet                       25,000.00  *
                                     (57,256.00)
Mark-up                                    1.40
Cost of Goods                         40,897.14

Withdrawal from Inventory              1,500.00
Mark-up                                    1.40
Expense                                1,071.43
```

THE COST OF GOODS SOLD CALCULATION FOR PAPER CLIP WAREHOUSE. THE INTERCOMPANY SALE OF SUPPLIES TO CORPORATE OFFICE IS ELIMINATED OR TREATED AS IF THE TRANSACTION NEVER OCCURRED, ACCORDING TO GAAP PRINCIPLES.

E. Matching, Expense Recognition - Allocation of intangible assets is the systematic expensing of those assets over the periods benefited. Intangible assets include the prepaid insurance, software licenses fees, and business licenses. For the first month of operation, beginning December 1, 20xx, the prepaid allocation is going to be based on the in-service date to ensure that the expenses are properly matched to the revenue that was generated for the period that operations began. It is important to note two dates in particular, the purchase date and the date the asset was placed in service. The software licenses were purchased on December 8; however, they were not used until December 10 when training started. Both the insurance and licenses were purchased on December 8; however, these costs are going to be applied to the date the company began operating.

Prepaid Expenses	Purchase Date	In-service date				Total	Allocation Period	Monthly Allocation Amount	December 20xx Allocation
Blanket Insurance	December 8, 20xx	December 1, 20xx	24,000.00			24,000.00	12	2,000.00	2,000.00
Software license fees	December 8, 20xx	December 10, 20xx	50,000.00			50,000.00	12	4,166.67	2,822.58
Business license	December 8, 20xx	December 1, 20xx		1,200.00	1,200.00	2,400.00	12	200.00	200.00
Total			74,000.00	1,200.00	1,200.00	76,400.00		6,366.67	5,022.58

ALLOCATION OF PAPER CLIP WAREHOUSE'S INTANGIBLE ASSETS. THE PURCHASE DATE AND THE SERVICE DATE OF THE ASSET ARE IMPORTANT CONSIDERATIONS WHEN DETERMINING THE APPROPRIATE ALLOCATION.

F. Matching, Expense Recognition - Depreciation of long-lived assets is the systematic expensing of those assets over their estimated useful lives. The purpose is two-fold: to match the revenue generated with those assets to the expense of the assets, and to decrease the asset value to fair value.

There are multiple depreciation methods: straight-line ((total cost − salvage value)/(estimated useful life)), declining or double declining balance ((2*straight line depreciation percent)*(book value at beginning of period-salvage value)-accumulated depreciation)), and sum of the year's digits (if the asset was expected to last for five years, the sum of the years' digits would be obtained by adding: 5 + 4 + 3 + 2 + 1 to get a total of 15, then each digit is divided by this sum to determine the percentage by which the asset should be depreciated each year, starting with the highest number in year 1), all of which are acceptable under GAAP. As with the allocation of prepaid expenses, depreciation begins on the date the asset was placed in service. The formula for the straight-line method used for our illustrative purposes is:

$$\text{Annual Depreciation Expense} = \frac{\text{Cost of Asset} + \text{Costs to make ready for intended use} - \text{Salvage Value}}{\text{Estimated Useful Life (years)}}$$

FORMULA FOR CALCULATING STRAIGHT-LINE DEPRECIATION

Depreciation is a significant challenge for accounting. Depreciation entries require a substantial amount of estimation, such as the useful life of the asset and what costs associated with the asset should be capitalized. Depreciation is an allowable deduction on the tax return of the company, and the method used for bookkeeping and taxes can be different. If the company chooses to use different depreciation methods, a large amount of bookkeeping and tax differences can be created. These differences require a great amount of disclosure and are typically handled by tax specialists.

Paper Clip Warehouse Fixed Asset Schedule	Estimated Useful Life - Years	Estimated Salvage Value	Purchase Date	In-service Date	Corporate - 100	East Coast 200	West Coast 300	Total Monthly Depreciation Expense
Furniture	7	0	12/05/20xx	12/10/20xx	10,000	20,000	45,000	
Monthly Depreciation - Furniture					119	238	536	893
December Depreciation Expense					81	161	363	
Computer Equipment	5	0	12/06/20xx	12/10/20xx	130,000	130,000	130,000	
Monthly Depreciation - Computer					2,167	2,167	2,167	6,500
December Depreciation Expense					1,468	1,468	1,468	
Building	39	0	12/04/20xx	12/04/20xx		1,000,000	2,500,000	
Monthly Depreciation - Building						2,137	5,342	7,479
December Depreciation Expense						1,861	4,653	
Parking Lot	20	0	12/04/20xx	12/04/20xx		300,000	750,000	
Monthly Depreciation - Parking Lot						1,250	3,125	4,375
December Depreciation Expense						1,089	2,722	
Parking Lot Repair	20	0	12/05/20xx	12/5/20xx		50,000		
Monthly Depreciation - Parking Lot						208		208
December Depreciation Expense						175		
Land	Forever		12/03/20xx		105,000	700,000	1,750,000	

ACCOUNTING FOR PAPER CLIP WAREHOUSE DEPRECIATION OF ASSETS. IN THIS CASE, WE HAVE USED THE STRAIGHT-LINE METHOD OF DEPRECIATION.

G. Matching, Expense Recognition – The December 31 payroll date paid employees up to December 24, 20xx. An additional 6 days of payroll must be accrued for December.

Payroll Accrual Calculation	Last Payroll	Number of days in pay period	Estimated Payroll per day	Number of days to accrue	Accrual to be recorded
Salaries	21,100	14	1,507	6	9,042.86
Wages	4,200	14	300	6	1,800.00
Payroll Tax	5,060	14	361	6	2,168.57

The Paper Clip Warehouse operates 7 days per week and is closed all major holidays. Staff is paid for holidays.

PAYROLL ACCRUAL FOR THE MONTH OF DECEMBER. BECAUSE THE FIRST PAYROLL PERIOD ONLY WENT THROUGH DECEMBER 24, 6 MORE DAYS OF PAYROLL MUST BE RECORDED AS EXPENSE TO ENSURE ALL OF THE PAYROLL RELATED TO 20XX IS INCLUDED IN THE FINANCIAL STATEMENTS.

H. Matching, Expense Recognition - Property taxes must be estimated. Management believes that annual property taxes will be $15,000 for the East Coast store and $18,000 for the West Coast store.

Location	Estimated Property Tax	Number of Months	Estimated Monthly Property Tax
East Coast	15,000	12	1,250
West Coast	18,000	12	1,500

ESTIMATED ANNUAL PROPERTY TAXES FOR PAPER CLIP WAREHOUSE STORE LOCATIONS. WE HAVE TO ESTIMATE THE ANNUAL PROPERTY TAX TO DETERMINE THE ESTIMATED MONTHLY PROPERTY TAX EXPENSE TO INCLUDE IN THE FINANCIAL STATEMENT.

I. Matching, Expense Recognition – Currently, the phone and utility bills for December have not been received for any location. Management estimates the electricity, water, sewer, and trash at $800 for 100, $3,200 for 200, and $2,800 for 300. The phone bills are estimated at $250 for 100, $900 for 200, and $650 for 300.

J. Matching, Expense Recognition - Payments on the note payable are due on the 5th of each month, with the first note due January 5, 20xx. Interest expense must be recorded in December.

K. Revenue recognition - Interest was earned on the $3,000,000 marketable securities account at 1.5% annual interest. Unrealized gains on the

▶ INTEREST CALCULATOR

Initial Deposit: $ 3000000
Interest Rate: 1 . 5 %
Months: 1
Compounding: Monthly
Ending Balance: $3,003,750.00

INTEREST EARNED ON THE MARKETABLE SECURITIES ACCOUNTS. THIS SHOWS THE ESTIMATED INTEREST EARNED FOR DECEMBER.

Amortization table for $10,000,000.00 borrowed on Dec 01, 2013

Month / Year	Payment	Principal Paid	Interest	Total	Balance
Jan. 2014	$179,686.91	$154,686.91	$25,000.00	$25,000.00	$9,845,313.09
Feb. 2014	$179,686.91	$155,073.62	$24,613.28	$49,613.28	$9,690,239.47
Mar. 2014	$179,686.91	$155,461.31	$24,225.60	$73,838.88	$9,534,778.16
April 2014	$179,686.91	$155,849.96	$23,836.95	$97,675.83	$9,378,928.20
May 2014	$179,686.91	$156,239.59	$23,447.32	$121,123.15	$9,222,688.61
June 2014	$179,686.91	$156,630.19	$23,056.72	$144,179.87	$9,066,058.43
July 2014	$179,686.91	$157,021.76	$22,665.15	$166,845.01	$8,909,036.67
Aug. 2014	$179,686.91	$157,414.31	$22,272.59	$189,117.61	$8,751,622.35
Sept. 2014	$179,686.91	$157,807.85	$21,879.06	$210,996.66	$8,593,814.50
Oct. 2014	$179,686.91	$158,202.37	$21,484.54	$232,481.20	$8,435,612.13
Nov. 2014	$179,686.91	$158,597.88	$21,089.03	$253,570.23	$8,277,014.26
Dec. 2014	$179,686.91	$158,994.37	$20,692.54	$274,262.76	$8,118,019.89
Jan. 2015	$179,686.91	$159,391.86	$20,295.05	$294,557.81	$7,958,628.03

AMORTIZATION TABLE FOR THE $10 MILLION STARTUP LOAN. INTEREST EXPENSE MUST BE RECORDED FOR DECEMBER, EVEN THOUGH THE FIRST PAYMENT IS NOT DUE UNTIL JANUARY.

long-term investments are $2,500. The estimated interest earned for December will be $1,875, because the account was not opened until the 15th. In today's world, the responsible accountant or treasury staff will log into the investment company portal to get the exact interest-earned figure.

L. Conservatism - The firewall invoice is going to be accrued until accounts payable can confirm the intent of the firewall with IT.

M. Matching, Expense Recognition – Management believes that the statutory income tax rate is going to be 15%.

All of the entries to close the books and prepare financial statements will be posted to the general ledger using the journal entry process. Some journal entries are going to be permanent, some will be reversed in the next month, and some will be "trued-up" when the final numbers are known. When you hear an accountant mention that the account balance will be trued-up, it means that estimated accruals are being made and when the final numbers are known, the account balance will be adjusted to include the final numbers. Permanent journal entries are expense allocations of intangible assets and depreciation of fixed assets, which require reconciliation at each accounting close. Journal entries to be reversed in the next month are accruals for expenses incurred in the current month, but the invoice will not be received until the next month. Expenses that will be "trued-up" when the final numbers are known are permanent entries that record liabilities on the balance sheet. These future liabilities include but are not limited to property taxes, income taxes, and warranties (if offered as part of the transaction). Just like any other expense, these future liabilities must be matched to the revenue that was generated.

The consolidated adjusted trial balance for the Paper Clip Warehouse is complete. From this point, financial statement preparation is a matter of formatting the balance sheet and income statement from the trial balance and calculating the statement of cash flows and retained earnings.

	Paper Clip Warehouse - Working Trial Balance							
	December 31, 20xx							
Account Code	Account Title	Corporate - 100	East Coast - 200	West Coast - 300	Unadjusted Consolidated Trial Balance	Adjustments		Consolidated
11100	Cash - Operating Corporate	13,985,600			13,985,600	(5,000,000)	A	8,985,600
11105	Cash - Operating - East Coast		43,900		43,900	(1,200)	A	42,700
11110	Cash - Operating - West Coast			(5,120)	(5,120)	(1,200)	A	(6,320)
11200	Cash - Investing				-	3,001,875	A&J	3,001,875
11300	Petty Cash				-	2,400	A	2,400
11400	Accounts Receivable		92,892	9,624	102,516			102,516
11410	Allowance for Doubtful Accounts				-	(1,538)	B	(1,538)
11420	Deposits	14,000			14,000			14,000
11430	Prepaid Expense	74,000	1,200	1,200	76,400	(5,023)	D	71,377
11500	Inventory		42,000	42,000	84,000	(41,969)	C	42,031
11600	Long Term Investments				-	2,002,500	A&J	2,002,500
12100	Furniture, Fixtures & Equipment (FFE)	140,000	150,000	175,000	465,000			465,000
12110	Accumulated Depreciation - FFE				-	(5,008)	E	(5,008)
12200	Building		1,000,000	2,500,000	3,500,000			3,500,000
12210	Accumulated Depreciation - Building				-	(6,514)	E	(6,514)
12300	Land	105,000	700,000	1,750,000	2,555,000			2,555,000
12400	Land Improvements		350,000	750,000	1,100,000			1,100,000
12410	Accumulated Depreciation - Land Improvements				-	(3,985)	E	(3,985)
21100	Trade Payable	(379,000)	(2,300,300)	(5,279,200)	(7,958,500)			(7,958,500)
21200	Salaries/Wages Payable				-	(13,011)	F	(13,011)
21300	Taxes Payable				-	31,184	G&L	31,184
21400	Accrued Liabilities				-	(13,600)	H&K	(13,600)
22000	Deferred Revenue		(75,000)		(75,000)			(75,000)
23000	Current Portion of Notes Payable	(833,333)			(833,333)			(833,333)
24000	Interest Payable				-	(25,000)	I	(25,000)
25000	Notes Payable	(9,166,667)			(9,166,667)			(9,166,667)
26000	Contingent Liabilities				-			-
27000	Due to/Due from	(1,500)		1,500	-			-
31000	Common Stock	(100,000)			(100,000)			(100,000)
32000	Additional Paid in Capital	(3,900,000)			(3,900,000)			(3,900,000)
33000	Retained Earnings				-			-
41000	Sales		(68,992)	(14,764)	(83,756)	1,500	C	(82,256)
41100	Sales Discounts				-			-
41110	Sales Returns & Allowances				-			-
51000	Purchases		10,000		10,000	40,897	C	50,897
52000	Freight In		50		50			50
61000	Salaries	10,000	5,000	6,100	21,100	9,043	F	30,143
61100	Wages	2,000	1,000	1,200	4,200	1,800	F	6,000
61150	Payroll Tax Expense	2,400	1,200	1,460	5,060	2,169	F	7,229
61200	Freight Out		50		50			50
61300	Rent	14,000			14,000			14,000
61400	Utilities				-	6,800	H	6,800
61500	Telephone				-	1,800	H	1,800
61600	Advertising		2,500	2,500	5,000			5,000
61700	Repairs and Maintenance			14,000	14,000	5,000	K	19,000
61800	Office Supplies	1,500			1,500	(429)	C	1,071
61900	Contract Labor		12,500	12,500	25,000			25,000
62000	Insurance				-	2,000	D	2,000
63000	Staffing Fees	32,000	32,000	32,000	96,000			96,000
64000	Licenses Fees				-	3,023	D	3,023
65000	Bad Debt Expense				-	1,538	B	1,538
67000	Depreciation Expense				-	15,507	E	15,507
67100	Interest Expense				-	25,000	I	25,000
67200	Property Tax Expense				-	2,750	G	2,750
67300	Gain/Loss on sale of assets				-			-
67350	Income Tax Expense				-	(33,934)	L	(33,934)
67400	Interest Income				-	(1,875)	J	(1,875)
67500	Unrealized Gain/Loss on Investments				-	(2,500)	J	(2,500)
	Check Figure	-	-	-	-	0		0

CONSOLIDATED ADJUSTED TRIAL BALANCE FOR THE PAPER CLIP WAREHOUSE, ONCE THIS IS FINAL, THE BULK OF THE WORK FOR FINANCIAL STATEMENT PREPERATION IS COMPLETE.

Here is the Paper Clip Warehouse December 31, 20xx, financial statements required by GAAP.

Paper Clip Warehouse
Balance Sheet
As of December 31, 20xx

Assets	
Current Assets	
Cash and Cash Equivalents	12,026,255
Net Receivables	100,978
Inventory	42,031
Deposits	14,000
Prepaid Expense	71,377
Deferred Tax Asset	33,934
Total Current Assets	12,288,575
Long Term Investments	2,002,500
Property, Plant and Equipment at cost	
Furniture and Fixtures	459,992
Building	3,493,486
Land	2,555,000
Land Improvements	1,096,015
Total Property Plant & Equipment at cost	7,604,493
Total Assets	21,895,568
Liabilities and Stockholders' Equity	
Current Liabilities	
Trade Payable	7,958,500
Salaries/Wages Payable	13,011
Taxes Payable	2,750
Accrued Liabilities	13,600
Deferred Revenue	75,000
Current Portion of Notes Payable	833,333
Interest Payable	25,000
Total Current Liabilities	8,921,195
Notes Payable	9,166,667
Stockholders' Equity	
Common Stock	100,000
Additional Paid in Capital	3,900,000
Retained Earnings	-
Current Year Net Loss	(192,293)
Total Stockholders' Equity	3,807,707
Total Liabilities and Stockholders' Equity	21,895,568

Paper Clip Warehouse
Income Statement
For the year ending December 31, 20xx

Revenues		
Sales	82,256	100%
Cost of Sales	50,947	62%
Gross Profit	31,309	38%
Expenses		
Salaries	30,143	37%
Wages	6,000	7%
Payroll Tax Expense	7,229	9%
Freight Out	50	0%
Rent	14,000	17%
Utilities	6,800	8%
Telephone	1,800	2%
Advertising	5,000	6%
Repairs and Maintenance	19,000	23%
Office Supplies	1,071	1%
Contract Labor	25,000	30%
Insurance	2,000	2%
Staffing Fees	96,000	117%
Licenses Fees	3,023	4%
Bad Debt Expense	1,538	2%
Depreciation Expense	15,507	19%
Interest Expense	25,000	30%
Property Tax Expense	2,750	3%
Total Expenses	261,911	318%
Operating Income	(230,602)	-280%
Non-Operating Income		
Interest Income	1,875	2%
Unrealized Gain/Loss on Investments	2,500	3%
Income Tax Provision	33,934	41%
Net Income (Loss)	(192,293)	-234%

CHAPTER 10 **123**

Paper Clip Warehouse
Statement of Stockholders' Equity
For the year ending December 31, 20xx

	Common Stock, $1 Par	Paid-in Capital in Excess of Par	Retained Earnings	Total Stockholders Equity
Balance on December 1	-	-	-	-
Issured Shares for Cash	100,000	3,900,000		4,000,000
Net Income			(192,293)	(192,293)
Balance on December 31	100,000	3,900,000	(192,293)	3,807,707

Paper Clip Warehouse
Statement of Cash Flows (Indirect)
For the year ending December 31, 20xx

Cash flows from operationg activities		
Net income / (Loss)		(192,293)
Add (Deduct) noncash effects on operating income		
Depreciation Expense	15,507	
Increase in accounts receivable	(100,978)	
Increase in inventory	(42,031)	
Increase in prepaids & deposits	(85,377)	
Increase in deferred tax asset	(33,934)	
Increase in long term investments	(2,002,500)	
Increase in accounts payable	7,958,500	
Increase in salaries payable	13,011	
Increase in accrued liabilities and other payables	13,600	
Increase in interest payable	25,000	
Increase in taxes payable	2,750	
Increase in deferred revenue	75,000	5,838,548
Net cash provided by operating activities		5,646,255
Cash flows from investing activities		
Increase of furniture, fixtures & Equipment	(465,000)	
Increase of Land	(2,555,000)	
Increase of Land Improvements	(1,100,000)	
Purchase of Buildings	(3,500,000)	
Net cash provided by investing activities		(7,620,000)
Cash flows from financing activities		
Proceeds from issuing stock	4,000,000	
Proceeds from long-term debt	10,000,000	
Net cash provided by financing activities		14,000,000
Net increase in cash		12,026,255
Cash balance at December 1, 20xx		-
Cash balance at December 31, 20xx		12,026,255

PAPER CLIP WAREHOUSE FINANCIAL STATEMENTS THAT ARE COMPLETED IN ACCORDANCE WITH GAAP.

Transaction initiation to inclusion on financial statement

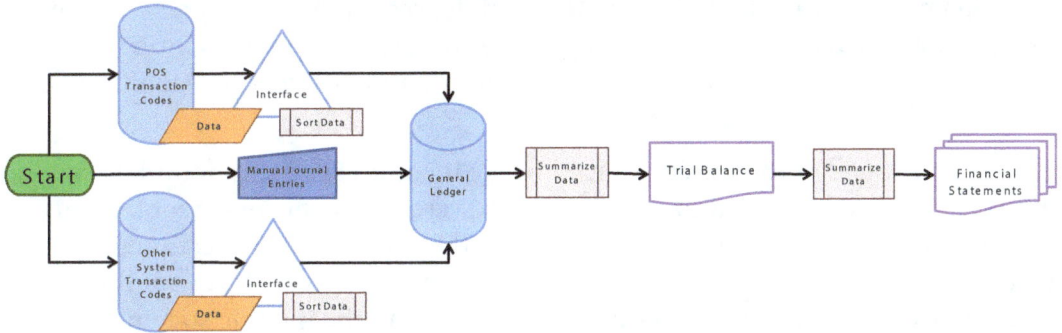

Basic transaction processing from initiation to inclusion on financial statements – Other system transaction codes include other accounting application modules, payroll systems and any system that generates data that is recorded to the general ledger.

Some final words – as you review these statements, take time to trace the line items back to the transactions we have been discussing. Consider that these transactions can occur many, many times during a single day within the accounting cycle. On the balance sheet, note the inclusion of a deferred tax asset. The astute reader would have observed that the Paper Clip Warehouse has a net loss for the first month of operations, which would generally result in a tax refund. Remember, a debit (positive) balance represents an asset, so we cannot leave this amount in the liability section. We performed an "off-book" memo entry, also known as a "top-side" entry, in our end-user financial statement application to reclass the $33,934 tax refund from the liability section to the asset section. Since this is the first month of operations for the company, there have been no prior tax payments made; therefore, no real refund is due to the company. Accounting for taxes is a specialized and complex area of accounting and requires the extreme accounting nerds. Additional details are far beyond the scope of this book, but I point it out to highlight the complexity of financial statement preparation.

Notice that the income statement "falls" out of the balance sheet. When we were recording journal entries, nominal accounts were offset with the real accounts on the balance sheet. For example, a credit to sales generally had a debit to cash or accounts receivable. A debit to an expense account generally had a credit to accounts payable or inventory. Also note, the only way the balance sheet will balance is with the current period profit or loss included as a component of owner's equity.

Calculating the statement of cash flow requires analysis of the changes in the ending balance sheet accounts. The beginning balance minus that ending balance equals the cash flow for the period. Then, an analysis of the source of cash is required. This is the first month of activity, so all of the beginning balances are zero.

The final piece of the financial statements is the footnote section. This is the section where you tell the financial statement users about the significant accounting policies used, including methods of depreciation you use, how inventory valuation is calculated, book to tax reconciliations, significant accounting estimates used by management, and any other information of material significance to a reader of the financial statement.

At the end of each fiscal year, all of the income statement nominal accounts are closed (zeroed out) and the profit is added (credit) or the loss is subtracted (debit) from the retained earnings account in the owners' equity section of the balance sheet. The financial statements for the new fiscal year start with the ending balances from the prior year on the balance sheet and the income statement with zero income and expense accounts. The income statement accounts will remain zero until the first transaction of the new accounting cycle is recorded.

To date, an accounting application cannot prepare financial statements in accordance with GAAP without human intervention. Because of the changing needs of users and the fluid nature of accounting rules and regulations that affect a company's reporting requirements, even the best designed accounting applications require trained accountants to properly prepare financial statements. Notice the format of the statements – these are just one example of multiple formats available to companies.

If you are still confused, it really is okay. Our simple example of one type of each transaction for the Paper Clip Warehouse got pretty complicated in a few places. Even with the automation of today's accounting packages, accounting is very much an interactive process and requires the full support and cooperation of all departments within an organization. No matter how small or remote an activity is within a business, it is going to affect accounting.

"What do accountants suffer from that ordinary people don't?"
Depreciation[143]

CHAPTER 11

- FRIGGIN' BEAN COUNTERS -
MANIPULATE AND MISSTATE FOR BETTER RESULTS?

Financial Statement Manipulation and Misstatements

Part of the inhumanity of the computer is that, once it is competently programmed and working smoothly, it is completely honest.

~ Isaac Asimov, American author and professor of biochemistry at Boston University[89]

Misstatement of financial results is either unintentional or intentional. An unintentional misstatement is considered an error. As long as humans are interacting with accounting applications, errors are unavoidable. An intentional misstatement is a manipulation of the financial results and is considered fraud. Financial statement fraud is never a random act; it is a deliberate manipulation of financial results in an attempt to benefit certain individuals and/or alter the decisions of the financial statement users. As we discussed in Chapter 3, there have been high profile corporate scandals that have highlighted the devastating affects of financial statement fraud.

Reasons to commit financial statement manipulation can be internal and external. External forces that could influence financial statement manipulations are loan covenants, minimum requirements to participate in contract bidding, investor expectations, the need to raise capital by selling bonds or additional stocks, or the pending sale of the company or its divisions. Loan covenants could require specific operating results that, if not met, could result in increased interest rates or repayment amounts. The company may not be granted additional loans or extensions. A company looking for competitive bids may only consider submissions from companies with specific operating results. Potential investors are driven by their own risk/reward profiles and publicly available information is the only way to determine the potential risk to investors. A company with a perceived higher risk may not attract investors. If the company is negotiating a sale for all or a portion of the business, purchase prices can be based on a multiple of earnings, which could incentivize manipulation of earnings to appear higher and increase the purchase price.

Corporate governance is not a new topic and has been part of the debate since the 1970's. Corporate governance refers to a system of structures, rights, duties, and obligations that direct and control corporations. Corporate governance for multilayered global companies is a challenge. Internal control structures and activities that work in one part of the world may be illegal in another. Complex organizational structures are created to address fierce global competition and the expectations of all stakeholders. When a company has multiple layers of management without clear guidelines and expectations, goals and objectives are poorly communicated and unclear, and a culture of being number one by any means creates complexities that make monitoring corporate governance difficult. When corporate governance is not monitored, incentives to generate fraudulent financial reporting are not mitigated with proper internal controls. Management override of the controls in place becomes easy to do. Information technology can make financial statement manipulation a simple matter to commit and difficult to detect. However, a well-designed information system can provide the tools to make early detection a viable solution.

Organizational culture is the behavior of the people and groups that are part of the company and includes values, ethics, visions, systems, beliefs, and habits. These behaviors influence interactions within the organization and with customers and other stakeholders. Organizational culture is a significant internal force that influences financial statement manipulation. When a financial statement misstatement has been identified, great care must be taken to determine if the misstatement is due to a deliberate manipulation of results or an innocent error. Organizational culture plays a primary role in creating incentives and justifications for deliberate manipulation of financial results. The company leadership sets and reinforces the organization's culture. Financial statement manipulation can become a daily activity for companies that have little regard for ethical values. The organizational culture should always demand excellence, but when a disproportionate emphasis is placed on exceeding projected operating budgets, an incentive for financial result manipulation is created.

The following is a list of potential indicators of financial statement manipulation based on organizational culture practices. These indicators are not all inclusive and are presented to demonstrate that everyday behaviors and attitudes cannot be dismissed. A solid partnership between IT and Accounting can be a great alliance in the prevention of financial statement manipulation.

Organization practices:

- When top executives create a culture of fear with anger and intimidation, which causes employees to not deliver bad news if it can be avoided.
- The CFO who is under threat of termination could adjust the numbers so that the results presented to the top executives are within expectations.
- When too much emphasis is placed on budget to actual variances, the budget dictates the financial statements.
- When salary increases, bonuses, and stock option grants are awarded based only on operating results, a significant incentive is created to manipulate financial results.

- When the CFO needs to have a project moved up in the project queue, quid pro quo deals are negotiated.
- One person has complete control of the financial reporting.
- The organizational structure is unreasonably complex, with multiple layers of management without any apparent need.

Accounting practices:

- A cookie jar is created by accruing a "future expense" on a monthly basis. The CFO decides to accrue $100 per month expense "just in case."
- Standard accruals are recorded without being reconciled or evaluated. If the company has trouble getting employee expense reports in a timely manner, a standard accrual can be established.
- Expenses and/or revenues are deferred by accruing and/or reversing entries each month to be reversed when the results would be more favorable.
- Actual results are adjusted to equal the budget.
- Expenses not budgeted are hidden within other transactions. Project costs that were underestimated for one project are added to a project that is under budget.
- There are aggressive capitalization policies at the company. Capitalization is recording expenses on the balance sheet as assets because there is a future benefit expected.
- Accounting standards are ignored or improperly applied. The company uses materiality as an excuse to not properly apply accounting standards or record journal entries that are required by GAAP. Materiality is the constraint that states the significance of an item should be considered when it is reported. An item is considered material when it would affect the decision of a reasonable user.
- Balance sheet accounts that have suspense, miscellaneous, or other in the account title and are vaguely defined on the chart of accounts are often used for cookie jars and other unsupported entries.
- Account balances do not conform to the normal and expected balance – assets and expenses should have a positive (debit) balance, while liabilities, owner's equity, and income should have negative (credit) balance. A liability account with a debit balance could indicate that fictitious revenue has been recorded.

Accounting application:

- Reports that do not include all accounts could be used to avoid reporting select financial results.
- The same journal entry is recorded and reversed each month.
- All users have access to all system functionality.
- One user has control of all the system functionality.
- Account reconciliations performed within the accounting application are not completed in a timely fashion.
- Journal entries are recorded to force the system reconciliation to balance.
- Journal entries posted prior to closing the books are adjusting actual results to the budget.
- There are significant manual workarounds for inadequate system functionality.

Human behavior indicators:

- Executive management is domineering and refuses to hear bad news.
- Coworkers are treated with disrespect or are verbally abused as a matter of course.
- Executive management promises that maximum bonuses are always awarded if targets are exceeded
- Employees appear to be living beyond their means.
- Auditors are not allowed access to all information.
- Management attitudes toward financial information are secretive or evasive.

U.S. GAAP and other recognized accounting frameworks provide sufficient guidance to ensure that financial statements are not misstated by a material amount. Legislation has been passed to enforce laws that require a company to implement and maintain a system of internal controls. Publicly traded companies are required to have an annual audit conducted by an independent auditing firm and are required to ensure that the financial statements present fairly the results of operations, in all material respects.

Paper Clip Warehouse Manipulations

Whoever is detected in a shameful fraud is ever after not believed even if they speak the truth.

~The Phaedra's, written by Plato 370 BC, dialog between Plato's main protagonist, Socrates, and Phaedrus[90]

The Paper Clip Warehouse has just completed its first year of operations. Financial statements were prepared based on information available from the accounting application and other closing procedures. Because of competing priorities when opening a business, all of the accounting application's functions were not fully implemented. The financial statements were prepared using an end-user computer application that was created by the CFO with a recognized commercially available spreadsheet application. It is the second week of the new fiscal year, and while the financial statements are completed, they have not been filed with the proper regulatory agencies.

Determining if financial statements are complete and correct is not an easy task. Determining if identified errors are deliberate manipulations of the results or simple mistakes is even more difficult. To illustrate the great care that must be taken when assessing a misstatement as a deliberate manipulation or an error, consider the impact of a contingent liability. Contingent liabilities are potential financial obligations that are dependent on the outcome of a future event. The conservatism constraint requires that when choosing between two solutions, the one that will be least likely to overstate assets and income should be chosen. If a contingent liability results in a financial obligation and the liability has not been recorded or disclosed, then the financial statements are not prepared in accordance with GAAP. GAAP requires that when notification of a potential contingent liability is received, a company must assess the likelihood of a potential future financial obligation as probable, reasonably possible, or remote. If a company believes that the outcome is probable and money will be owed, then the amount must be estimated and accrued. If the company believes that the outcome is reasonably possible or remote, they are required to disclose the situation in the financial statement footnotes.

During the renovation of the parking lot at the East Coast store, Sonny Otis decided to save some money and act as the contractor of record. There was a vat of tar heating up out of public view which was difficult for the public to access and clearly marked to stay away. It was a cold evening when a traveler and his canine companion were looking for a warm place to stay. The warmth from the vat of tar was inviting, and the dog got too close. Unfortunately, signs are ignored and accidents happen. During the second week of January, Sonny Otis received notice of a pending lawsuit. Notification of the pending lawsuit qualifies as a contingent liability because there is a potential of a monetary liability that is dependent on other events, such as a judge's ruling, willingness of the claimant to settle, and the jury verdict of liability and awards.

The lawsuit was not considered during the initial preparation of the year-end financial statements. So what does this mean: Are the financial statements misstated? Is there a deliberate manipulation of financial results? Does it make a difference that the notice was received after year end? These are very relevant questions that must receive in-depth consideration.

- Does it make a difference that the notice was received after year end? Since the notification was received prior to the financial statements being made public, the impact of the notification is evaluated as a subsequent event. A subsequent event is defined as a material event that occurs after the end of the accounting period and before the publication of the financial statements. Because of the matching principle, we must consider the impact of the lawsuit notification in conjunction with the events that occurred during the accounting cycle that the prepared financial statements represent.

- Are the financial statements misstated? It depends on whether Accounting has a procedure in place that questions management about subsequent events and contingent liabilities at each period end. Public companies have a disclosure committee that meets quarterly to discuss such events. If none were known by management, then the financial statements prepared could be misstated, but it would be considered an error. If management did know and deliberately did not tell Accounting, then the financial statements are considered manipulated and fraudulent.

- Is there a deliberate manipulation of financial results? It depends – if Sonny Otis knew of the pending lawsuit and said nothing, then the financial statements are deliberately manipulated and are fraudulent. If the attorney told Sonny that an unfavorable outcome was probable and Sonny told Accounting that it was reasonably possible, then the financial statements are deliberately manipulated and fraudulent. A contingent liability that is reasonably possible requires disclosure in the financial statement notes; if the likelihood is probable, then the amount must be estimated and accrued.

For our financial statement presentation, it has been determined that the probability of an unfavorable outcome is remote, so the reporting requirements are to add a footnote disclosure. Footnote disclosures have little impact on the information systems and were not included in the previous examples. Since the determination of an unfavorable outcome is remote and was determined before the financial statements were issued, we would update the footnotes to include the details of the pending lawsuit. At that point, our financial statements are not misstated. If we choose not to update the footnotes, that would be a deliberate manipulation.

Contrary to popular belief, management is responsible for the financial statements, not accounting. Let's assume that Sonny Otis is a real bastard, refuses to hear bad news, and knows very little about accounting except that cash is king, threatens employees by yelling and firing on the spot, lives way beyond his means with multiple houses, vacations, private planes, and yachts, and has the company pay shopping expenses for his family. Sonny Otis instructed the CFO to issue checks to pay $105,000 for the vacant land and the $7,000,000 purchase price of the East and West Coast stores prior to year end. The week after accounts payable is closed for the year, the CFO realizes that he forgot to have the checks issued and is afraid he will be fired if Sonny finds out. At this point, the CFO must make a choice: he can have IT reopen Accounts Payable, face Sonny, and risk being fired, or he can quietly issue checks and adjust the balance sheet in the end-user application. If he adjusts the balance sheet by adding accounts Cash-Other, an asset, and Accrued Liabilities-Other, a liability, who will know? Cash-Other will reduce cash with a credit and is added to the cash and cash equivalents line item, and Accrued Liabilities-Other will reduce the liabilities and is added to Trade Payables. Looks good right? The CFO presents the manipulated balance sheet to Sonny and saves his job!

Paper Clip Warehouse
Balance Sheet
As of December 31, 20xx

Correct		Manipulated/Misstated	
Assets		Assets	
Current Assets		Current Assets	
Cash and Cash Equivalents	12,026,255	Cash and Cash Equivalents	4,921,255
Net Receivables	100,978	Net Receivables	100,978
Inventory	42,031	Inventory	42,031
Deposits	14,000	Deposits	14,000
Prepaid Expense	71,377	Prepaid Expense	71,377
Deferred Tax Asset	33,934	Deferred Tax Asset	33,934
Total Current Assets	12,288,575	Total Current Assets	5,183,575
Long Term Investments	2,002,500	Long Term Investments	2,002,500
Property, Plant and Equipment at cost		Property, Plant and Equipment at cost	
Furniture and Fixtures	459,992	Furniture and Fixtures	459,992
Building	3,493,486	Building	3,493,486
Land	2,555,000	Land	2,555,000
Land Improvements	1,096,015	Land Improvements	1,096,015
Total Property Plant & Equipment at cost	7,604,493	Total Property Plant & Equipment at cost	7,604,493
Total Assets	21,895,568	Total Assets	14,790,568
Liabilities and Stockholders' Equity		Liabilities and Stockholders' Equity	
Current Liabilities		Current Liabilities	
Trade Payable	7,958,500	Trade Payable	853,500
Salaries/Wages Payable	13,011	Salaries/Wages Payable	13,011
Taxes Payable	2,750	Taxes Payable	2,750
Accrued Liabilities	13,600	Accrued Liabilities	13,600
Deferred Revenue	75,000	Deferred Revenue	75,000
Current Portion of Notes Payable	833,333	Current Portion of Notes Payable	833,333
Interest Payable	25,000	Interest Payable	25,000
Total Current Liabilities	8,921,195	Total Current Liabilities	1,816,195
Notes Payable	9,166,667	Notes Payable	9,166,667
Stockholders' Equity		Stockholders' Equity	
Common Stock	100,000	Common Stock	100,000
Additional Paid in Capital	3,900,000	Additional Paid in Capital	3,900,000
Retained Earnings	–	Retained Earnings	–
Current year net loss	(192,293)	Current year net loss	(192,293)
Total Stockholders' Equity	3,807,707	Total Stockholders' Equity	3,807,707
Total Liabilities and Stockholders' Equity	21,895,568	Total Liabilities and Stockholders' Equity	14,790,568

ADJUSTED BALANCE SHEET. THE CFO MISSTATES THE FINANCIAL STATEMENTS BY MISALLOCATING FUNDS TO HIDE HIS MISTAKE.

This entry will have to be included in the statement of cash flows, but Sonny is not concerned about the statement of cash flows or the income statement. In fact, Sonny only cares about the amount of cash in the bank and the profit/loss (P&L) statement. A P&L statement and an income statement are terms that are often used interchangeably. In the context of the financial statements, the income statement reflects the company performance for a stated period of time and is prepared in conformance to GAAP. A P&L statement is an operational statement; it only presents revenues and expenses related to operations.

Sonny Otis has reviewed the income statement and is not at all happy with a $192,203 loss for the period. One of the loan covenants requires a gross profit percentage of at least 40%, and the store managers were each promised a one-time bonus of $10,000 for meeting that percentage.

Sonny used private funds to purchase a private jet for $10,000,000 that will be used primarily for family vacations, but he has instructed the CFO to charge it to the company since a small portion will be used for company travel. Sonny insists that the contract labor and staffing fees are capitalized as startup costs and promises the CFO additional staff if the numbers are "right." The CFO knows that if he does not do what Sonny requests, he will be fired. So he updates his resume and proceeds. Remember, in double-entry bookkeeping the debits must equal credits, so these manipulations have to be carefully thought out to ensure that the balance sheet balances and that the income statement flows from the balance sheet.

Sonny uses his calculator to decide what the revenue number should be to be in compliance with the loan covenant. An additional $3,000 in revenue will get the gross profit percentage to 40% as required by the loan covenant. The offset to the $3,000 will be added to Accounts Receivable - Other. The contract labor and staffing fees have been added to a Prepaid-Other account. Sonny Otis, forcing the addition of the entire cost of the plane to the books is fraud! The CFO understands the concept of the GAAP Economic Entity assumption and is trying to hide the private plane by adding it to the building asset and long-term notes payable accounts. When the fake $3,000 was added, the store managers qualified for the $10,000 bonuses each; however, the CFO decides not to accrue the $20,000 in bonuses for 20xx because he believes the $20,000 amount is not material and the auditors will catch the fake revenue. The newly stated balance sheet and Income Statement are presented with the correct versions for the Paper Clip Warehouse.

Paper Clip Warehouse
Balance Sheet
As of December 31, 20xx

Correct		Manipulated/Misstated	
Assets		**Assets**	
Current Assets		Current Assets	
Cash and Cash Equivalents	12,026,255	Cash and Cash Equivalents	4,921,255
Net Receivables	100,978	Net Receivables	103,978
Inventory	42,031	Inventory	42,031
Deposits	14,000	Deposits	14,000
Prepaid Expense	71,377	Prepaid Expense	192,377
Deferred Tax Asset	33,934	Deferred Tax Asset	33,934
Total Current Assets	12,288,575	Total Current Assets	5,307,575
Long Term Investments	2,002,500	Long Term Investments	2,002,500
Property, Plant and Equipment at cost		Property, Plant and Equipment at cost	
Furniture and Fixtures	459,992	Furniture and Fixtures	459,992
Building	3,493,486	Building	13,493,486
Land	2,555,000	Land	2,555,000
Land Improvements	1,096,015	Land Improvements	1,096,015
Total Property Plant & Equipment at cost	7,604,493	Total Property Plant & Equipment at cost	17,604,493
Total Assets	21,895,568	Total Assets	24,914,568
Liabilities and Stockholders' Equity		**Liabilities and Stockholders' Equity**	
Current Liabilities		Current Liabilities	
Trade Payable	7,958,500	Trade Payable	853,500
Salaries/Wages Payable	13,011	Salaries/Wages Payable	13,011
Taxes Payable	2,750	Taxes Payable	2,750
Accrued Liabilities	13,600	Accrued Liabilities	13,600
Deferred Revenue	75,000	Deferred Revenue	75,000
Current Portion of Notes Payable	833,333	Current Portion of Notes Payable	833,333
Interest Payable	25,000	Interest Payable	25,000
Total Current Liabilities	8,921,195	Total Current Liabilities	1,816,195
Notes Payable	9,166,667	Notes Payable	19,166,667
Stockholders' Equity		Stockholders' Equity	
Common Stock	100,000	Common Stock	100,000
Additional Paid in Capital	3,900,000	Additional Paid in Capital	3,900,000
Retained Earnings	-	Retained Earnings	-
Current year net loss	(192,293)	Current year net loss	(68,293)
Total Stockholders' Equity	3,807,707	Total Stockholders' Equity	3,931,707
Total Liabilities and Stockholders' Equity	21,895,568	Total Liabilities and Stockholders' Equity	24,914,569

Paper Clip Warehouse
Income Statement
For the year ending December 31, 20xx

Correct			Manipulated/Misstated		
Revenues			**Revenues**		
Sales	82,256	100%	Sales	85,256	100%
Cost of Sales	50,947	62%	Cost of Sales	50,947	60%
Gross Profit	31,309	38%	Gross Profit	34,309	40%
Expenses			**Expenses**		
Salaries	30,143	37%	Salaries	30,143	35%
Wages	6,000	7%	Wages	6,000	7%
Payroll Tax Expense	7,229	9%	Payroll Tax Expense	7,229	8%
Freight Out	50	0%	Freight Out	50	0%
Rent	14,000	17%	Rent	14,000	16%
Utilities	6,800	8%	Utilities	6,800	8%
Telephone	1,800	2%	Telephone	1,800	2%
Advertising	5,000	6%	Advertising	5,000	6%
Repairs and Maintenance	19,000	23%	Repairs and Maintenance	19,000	22%
Office Supplies	1,071	1%	Office Supplies	1,071	1%
Contract Labor	25,000	30%	Contract Labor	-	0%
Insurance	2,000	2%	Insurance	2,000	2%
Staffing Fees	96,000	117%	Staffing Fees	-	0%
Licenses Fees	3,023	4%	Licenses Fees	3,023	4%
Bad Debt Expense	1,538	2%	Bad Debt Expense	1,538	2%
Depreciation Expense	15,507	19%	Depreciation Expense	15,507	18%
Interest Expense	25,000	30%	Interest Expense	25,000	29%
Property Tax Expense	2,750	3%	Property Tax Expense	2,750	3%
Total Expenses	261,911	318%	Total Expenses	140,911	165%
Operating Income	(230,602)	-280%	Operating Income	(106,602)	-125%
Non-Operating Income			**Non-Operating Income**		
Interest Income	1,875	2%	Interest Income	1,875	2%
Unrealized Gain/Loss on Investments	2,500	3%	Unrealized Gain/Loss on Investments	2,500	3%
Income Tax Provision	33,934	41%	Income Tax Provision	33,934	40%
Net Income (Loss)	(192,293)	-234%	Net Income (Loss)	(68,293)	-80%

MISSTATED ADJUSTED BALANCE SHEET AND INCOME STATEMENT. THE CFO MORE SERIOUSLY MISSTATES THE FINANCIAL STATEMENTS UNDER ORDERS FROM THE CEO.

Just by looking, the manipulated/misstated statements look perfectly reasonable, and no one is the wiser. Sonny thinks the CFO is crazy and does not know anything about business, when the truth is, Sonny knows nothing about GAAP. Sonny had the CFO move the contract labor and the recruiting fees to the balance sheet because he called them startup costs. GAAP defines startup costs as one-time activities that an entity undertakes when it opens a new facility, introduces a new product or service, conducts business in a new territory or with a new class of customer or beneficiary, initiates a new process in an existing facility, or commences some new operation.[91] Prior to 1998, business entities were allowed to capitalize these costs and amortize them over a set period. As of December 15, 1998, these costs are required to be expensed as incurred. Today, significant differences exist between tax and accounting treatments for handling startup costs. For tax purposes, a portion of startup costs can be deducted in the first year and amortized over a period of 180 months, beginning with the month in which your business opens.

The matching principle clearly requires that the $20,000 bonus for the managers be accrued. By not accruing this amount, the CFO made the decision that including the $20,000 would have no impact on the decision of the financial statement users, and therefore including it did not matter. Materiality is defined as considering the significance of an item. An item is considered material when it would affect the decision of a reasonable user. Based on this definition, materiality can be applied to transaction amounts, account balances, and footnote disclosures. There is no accounting guidance that quantifies materiality, so the CFO may be right in not accruing the $20,000. The materiality concept creates a lot of ambiguity, which is generally resolved through agreement between management and the auditors. Who's to say what will affect the decision of a reasonable user? Two equally reasonable users may conclude differently if an item is presented at $1,000 as opposed to $10,000. The decision for one user is the same at $10,000 and $1,000, but for the other, $10,000 is going to change their decision. However, materiality should never be used as an excuse for not properly accounting for transactions.

There is a lot of human intervention in the preparation of financial statements, and we know there is nothing a computer can do to stop these types of manipulations. GAAP allows for a significant amount of management estimation in an attempt to "fairly present" the financial statements and many times provides insufficient guidance on how to calculate the estimates. So, how will the misstatements that Sonny made be identified? Much to the irritation and annoyance of management, accounting, and IT, the auditors are on the way. I hope this example has illustrated the need for financial statement audits.

An auditor is having a hard time sleeping and goes to see the doctor. The doctor asks, "Have you tried counting sheep?" The auditor says, "that's the problem, when you make a mistake I spend three hours performing additional procedures, writing the report and making recommendations."

CHAPTER 12

- FRIGGIN' BEAN COUNTERS -
WE THOUGHT THE AUDITORS WERE KIND OF NERDY

Why did the auditor cross the road?
Because he looked in the file and that's what they did last year.[92]

Auditing is a systematic examination of data, records, processes, and operational performance (financial, efficiency, and effectiveness) of a company for a stated purpose. According to the *Principles of Accountancy, American Bookkeeping Series:*

> …auditing is the art of examining books, records, accounts and the business interests with a view to discovering the actual condition. In any auditing the auditor perceives and recognizes the propositions before him for examination, collects evidence, evaluates the same and on this basis formulates his judgment, which is communicated through his audit report. An auditor is employed, ordinarily, (1) to detect fraud; (2) to prove the mechanical and mathematical accuracy of books; (3) to discover points in which the books do not conform to the principles of accountancy; (4) to exhibit the true condition of a business; (5) to make recommendations with a view to improvement. The purpose is then to give an opinion on the adequacy of controls (financial and otherwise) within an environment they audit, to evaluate and improve the effectiveness of risk management, control, and governance processes." [93]

An audit can be formal or informal. An informal audit can be as straightforward as the cash-receipts clerk reviewing the accounts receivable posting to ensure that all of the payments were applied to the correct customer, the line manager inspecting every 10th finished product to ensure that it is properly assembled, or the systems analyst reviewing the interface to ensure that the daily activity posted correctly. These are tasks that are performed daily as part of normal job duties without giving them much thought, but mentioning the word audit is enough to strike fear in the most seasoned manager. Most of this fear comes from a lack of understanding of the audit process.

A formal audit is a planned and documented activity that is performed by an objective, independent third party referred to as an auditor. The independent auditor is free from control, influence, and support of others.[94] The independent third party can be an external firm hired by the company or an internal auditor, if the company has an Internal Audit department.

External Audits

There are many reasons why a company may engage an external auditing firm to examine the books and records. A company that is publicly traded (stock sold on a recognized exchange) is required to have the financial statements audited annually by an external audit firm. The audit committee of the company's board of directors has primary responsibility for the selection of the audit firm. In a publicly traded company, the board of directors' report to the stockholders, and the audit committee is a subset of board members who do not work for the company. The audit must be complete prior to the public release of the financial statements.

A financial statement audit has specific objectives that are achieved through investigation, examination, and evaluation of evidence. The goal of the audit is for the audit firm to express an opinion (the report) on whether or not the financial statements are fairly presented in all material respects. In other words, do the financial statements reflect what is actually going on in the company? The auditor's report is included with the published financial statements. There is that word "material" again. Remember, an item is considered material when it would affect the decision of a reasonable user. Now we have auditors, along with the CFO and management, determining what will affect the decision of a reasonable user.

The first line of the standard audit report reads, "We have audited the accompanying balance sheet of ABC Company, Inc. (the "Company") as of December 31, 20XX, and the related statements of income, retained earnings, and cash flows for the year then ended."[14] The financial statement audit is going to focus on the balance sheet. Remember, the balance sheet is the financial statement that shows, in a monetary unit, what the business owns (assets), what it owes (liabilities), and the residual value (owner's equity) of the business. If the balance sheet is correct and properly supported, the income statement, cash flow statement, and statement of stockholder's equity are also going to be correct. This is always true, because posting original transactions in a double-entry bookkeeping system requires a minimum of two accounts. At least one real account will be used (remember, real accounts are the balance sheet accounts), with the offsetting entries to another real account or a nominal account (income statement). For example, see the table below.

Original Transaction	Balance Sheet	Offsetting entry
Sale for cash	Cash (Debit)	Revenue (Credit)
Sale on account	Accounts Receivable (Debit)	Revenue (Credit)
Purchase on account	Accounts Payable (Credit)	Expense (Debit)
Purchase for cash	Cash (Credit)	Expense (Debit)
Purchase of inventory	Inventory (Debit)	Accounts Payable (Credit)
Payments from customers	Accounts Receivable (Credit)	Cash (Debit)

TYPICAL DEBITS AND CREDITS FOR SPECIFIC TRANSACTIONS

The only time you will see a debit and credit entry to the income statement is to reclassify expense or income transactions from one account, or department or cost center to another.

Generally Accepted Audit Standards

As with GAAP, there is a significant amount of audit guidance called the Generally Accepted Audit Standards (GAAS). GAAS is a set of standards used by external auditors when conducting financial statement audits. These standards are intended to ensure the accuracy and consistency of auditor actions and the verifiability of the auditor's reports. GAAS has a total of ten standards: three general standards that apply to the competency and independence of the auditor, three standards of fieldwork that are related to the auditor actually going to the client site to gather information, and four reporting standards that tell the auditor what to include in the report. GAAS was the responsibility of the AICPA until SOX created the Public Company Accounting Oversight Board (PCAOB). The PCAOB is a non-profit corporation established by Congress to oversee the audits of public companies in order to protect investors and the public interest by promoting informative, accurate, and independent audit reports. The PCAOB is directed by the Sarbanes-Oxley Act of 2002 to establish auditing and related professional practice standards for registered public accounting firms to follow in the preparation and issuance of audit reports.

These GAAS standards are codified in AU Section 150, applicable to audits of non-public companies, and have been included in many of the standards issued by the PCAOB.

General

- The auditor must maintain independence in mental attitude in all matters related to the audit.
- The auditor must have adequate technical training and proficiency to perform the audit.
- The auditor must exercise due professional care during the performance of the audit and the preparation of the report.

Standards of Field Work

- The auditor must adequately plan the work and must properly supervise any assistants.
- The auditor must obtain a sufficient understanding of the entity and its environment, including its internal controls, to assess the risk of material misstatement of the financial statements whether due to error or fraud, and to design the nature, timing, and extent of further audit procedures.
- The auditor must obtain sufficient, appropriate audit evidence by performing audit procedures to afford a reasonable basis for an opinion regarding the financial statements under audit.

Standards of Reporting

- The auditor must state in the auditor's report whether the financial statements are presented in accordance with generally accepted accounting principles.

- The auditor must identify in the auditor's report those circumstances in which such principles have not been consistently observed in the current period in relation to the preceding period.

- When the auditor determines that informative disclosures are not reasonably adequate, the auditor must state so in the auditor's report.

- In the auditor's report, the auditor must either express an opinion regarding the financial statements taken as a whole, or state that an opinion cannot be expressed. When the auditor cannot express an overall opinion, the auditor should state the reasons in the auditor's report. In all cases where an auditor's name is associated with financial statements, the auditor should clearly indicate the character of the auditor's work, if any, and the degree of responsibility the auditor is taking, in the auditor's report.[96]

When a company issues financial statements in conformity with GAAP or IFRS, embodied within the financial statements are an interrelated, complex set of management assertions. The audit shorthand is E/O, V/A, R/O, C, and P/D, and according to the audit guidance, the assertions mean:

- Assets exist (E) and Liabilities occur (O) to acquire assets;

- Assets are properly valued (V) and are expensed using an appropriate allocation (A) method;

- The company has the right (R) to convert assets to cash and an obligation (O) to settle the liabilities;

- All transactions that occurred in the reporting period have been included in the financial statements so that they are complete (C);

- The financial statements are properly presented (P), and all necessary disclosures (D) have been made.[97]

These assertions become the basis for every financial statement audit. The auditors design tests to confirm that management assertions are correct at the transaction level, account balance level, and for the financial statement as a whole. The auditor will classify transactions into those that are significant for the company and those that are not. Transaction classes include revenue and expenses, such as cost of goods sold, nonrecurring transactions, purchase transactions, etc. The significance of a class of transactions is dependent on the products and/or services the company sells and auditor judgment. Revenue and cash will be significant for a company that strictly engages in services for cash. Cost of goods sold will be significant for a company that has a lot of inventory but will be insignificant for a services company that may offer discounted supplies as part of a services contract. For each class of transaction, management is asserting that the transaction has occurred and is valid, is accurately and completely recorded, and is properly classified and included in the correct accounting period.

It is the auditor's responsibility to obtain sufficient evidence to support the opinion in the audit report. Since it is not possible to test 100% of all activity occurring during the accounting period, the auditor will design tests that utilize a risk approach and sampling methods based on the risk that will provide evidence. Tests that are performed by auditors are: 1) risk assessment; 2) test of controls; and 3) substantive tests of transactions, which includes analytical procedures and tests of details of balances.

Risk assessment procedures and tests of controls are done during the audit planning. The auditor will evaluate corporate culture, competency of management and the accounting staff, the environment in which the entity operates, internal controls, and other areas the auditor feels are necessary to determine the most likely places a material misstatement could occur in the financial statements. (There's that word "material" again!) The outcome of the risk assessment and tests of controls determines where the auditors are going to spend their time, what types of tests they will perform, and how much sampling they will do.

Analytical procedures are the comparisons of recorded amounts to expectations developed by the auditor. These expectations are developed during the audit planning, and the comparisons are done during fieldwork. This test can provide evidence of possible misstatements or confirm that the recorded amounts are correct.

Tests of details of balances focus on validating the ending account balances in the general ledger. This testing generally focuses on significant account balances, subject to management estimates or accounts with unusual activity.

Audit of the Paper Clip Warehouse

Now that we are assuming Sonny Otis is a bastard and the CFO is afraid of losing his job, how will the external auditors determine that the financial statements have been misstated? Planning the audit is an important first step. For the year-end financial statement audit, the external auditors will perform procedures that will assist in assessing the audit risk. Audit risk is the risk that errors or intentional misstatements (fraud) will not be discovered. As part of the audit planning, the external auditors will perform interviews with select senior managers, and the CEO will be one of them. They will ask questions that will allow them to assess the management style and ethical makeup of the senior managers.

The external auditors will perform testing on the information systems, including the accounting application and all revenue production or tracking systems. Auditors like testing information systems because the extent of testing is reduced. Effective information system controls greatly reduce the risk of a misstatement in the financial statements and allow reduced testing of manual review controls.

Once a computer is programed correctly, it will execute with the same accuracy each time. A typical test of an IT system generally calls for a sample of one of each transaction type. The transaction selected will be followed from the initiation point, which could be sales, journal entries, purchases, inventory, etc., to its inclusion on the financial statements. If the transaction type tested is found to have processed through the information systems as expected, then no further testing is necessary.

The external auditors have completed the planning, and now they know that the financial statement module of the accounting system has not been fully implemented and Sonny Otis appears to be of questionable ethics. As a result, they are assessing the audit risk as high. The higher the assessed audit risk is, the more detailed testing the auditors are going to do.

The CFO provides the auditors with the following trial balance from the end-user financial statement preparation application.

	Paper Clip Warehouse - Working Trial Balance						
	December 31, 20xx						
Account Code	Account Title	Corporate - 100	East Coast - 200	West Coast - 300	Unadjusted Consolidated Trial Balance	Adjustments	Consolidated
11100	Cash - Operating Corporate	13,985,600			13,985,600	(5,000,000) A	8,985,600
11105	Cash - Operating - East Coast		43,900		43,900	(1,200) A	42,700
11110	Cash - Operating - West Coast			(5,120)	(5,120)	(1,200) A	(6,320)
11200	Cash - Investing				-	3,001,875 A&J	3,001,875
11300	Petty Cash				-	2,400 A	2,400
11510	Cash - Other					(7,105,000)	(7,105,000)
11400	Accounts Receivable		92,892	9,624	102,516		102,516
11405	Accounts Receivable - Other					3,000	3,000
11410	Allowance for Doubtful Accounts				-	(1,538) B	(1,538)
11420	Deposits	14,000			14,000		14,000
11430	Prepaid Expense	74,000	1,200	1,200	76,400	(5,023) D	71,377
11435	Prepaid - Other					121,000 D	121,000
15500	Inventory		42,000	42,000	84,000	(41,969) C	42,031
11600	Long Term Investments				-	2,002,500 A&J	2,002,500
12100	Furniture, Fixtures & Equipment (FFE)	140,000	150,000	175,000	465,000		465,000
12110	Accumulated Depreciation - FFE				-	(5,008) E	(5,008)
12200	Building		1,000,000	2,500,000	3,500,000	10,000,000	13,500,000
12210	Accumulated Depreciation - Building				-	(6,514) E	(6,514)
12300	Land	105,000	700,000	1,750,000	2,555,000		2,555,000
12400	Land Improvements		350,000	750,000	1,100,000		1,100,000
12410	Accumulated Depreciation - Land Improvements				-	(3,985) E	(3,985)
21100	Trade Payable	(379,000)	(2,300,300)	(5,279,200)	(7,958,500)		(7,958,500)
21105	Payable - Other					7,105,000	7,105,000
21200	Salaries/Wages Payable				-	(13,011) F	(13,011)
21300	Taxes Payable				-	31,184 G&I	31,184
21400	Accrued Liabilities				-	(13,600) H&I	(13,600)
22000	Deferred Revenue		(75,000)		(75,000)		(75,000)
23000	Current Portion of Notes Payable	(833,333)			(833,333)		(833,333)
24000	Interest Payable				-	(25,000) I	(25,000)
25000	Notes Payable	(9,166,667)			(9,166,667)	(10,000,000)	(19,166,667)
26000	Contingent Liabilities				-		-
27000	Due to/Due from	(1,500)		1,500	-		-
31000	Common Stock	(100,000)			(100,000)		(100,000)
32000	Additional Paid in Capital	(3,900,000)			(3,900,000)		(3,900,000)
33000	Retained Earnings				-		-
41000	Sales		(68,992)	(14,764)	(83,756)	1,500 C	(82,256)
41100	Sales Discounts				-	(3,000)	(3,000)
41110	Sales Returns & Allowances				-		-
51000	Purchases		10,000		10,000	40,897 C	50,897
52000	Freight In		50		50		50
61000	Salaries	10,000	5,000	6,100	21,100	9,043 F	30,143
61100	Wages	2,000	1,000	1,200	4,200	1,800 F	6,000
61150	Payroll Tax Expense	2,400	1,200	1,460	5,060	2,169 F	7,229
61200	Freight Out		50		50		50
61300	Rent	14,000			14,000		14,000
61400	Utilities				-	6,800 H	6,800
61500	Telephone				-	1,800 H	1,800
61600	Advertising		2,500	2,500	5,000		5,000
61700	Repairs and Maintenance			14,000	14,000	5,000 K	19,000

Trial balance provided to the auditors. It was generated from the CFO's desktop.

The auditors have decided that they will review any balance sheet account balances greater than plus or minus $5 million and the sales and cost of goods sold income statement accounts.

The first evidence the auditors obtained was a chart of accounts from the accounting application, which they compared to the trial balance. They immediately questioned the CFO about the discrepancies. The answer provided was that the accounting application was undergoing maintenance and he did not have the time to get the accounts added. It's easy to verify the seemingly plausible story. The next tests they performed were on Cash, Cash-Other, Building, Trade Payable, Payable-Other, and Notes Payable. The evidence the auditors asked for included the reconciliations and supporting documentation for selected transactions. Supporting documentation can include system-generated audit trails and transaction logs, sales receipts, PO's, and shipping and receiving documents. The auditors could also physically inspect and observe any asset, such as observing inventory counts and visiting buildings.

As the supporting documents are reviewed, the audit approach will be to trace the transactions to the financial statements and ask questions that will begin to lead to potential audit adjustments. The reclassification of the contract labor and staffing fees could be identified when the accounts payable is reviewed and the auditors question why these expenses were recorded as prepaid.

When the building asset account is reviewed because the ending balance is greater than $5 million, the auditors will question why the plane was booked here. They will ask for support related to the business needs and other proof to support the plane's inclusion. The CFO and Sonny could forge a third-party note payable to the company for the plane. The auditors can confirm the validity of the note payable with the lender. If Sonny refuses to allow the auditors to talk with the lender, that would be called a scope limitation by the auditors. When questioned about the Cash-Other, the CFO explained that the checks were written and sent out on December 31st, but because of some balancing problems they had with the system, the entry was made to a separate account. Again, it's easy to verify the seemingly plausible story.

So what now? Are these misstatements material? Would they change the decision of a financial statement user? The plane is currently in the building account, offsetting a note payable. Could Sonny Otis lie and say the plane is 100% business-related and that accounting recorded it wrong? What about the $3,000 – remember, it was recorded as revenue because the loan covenant required a 40% gross profit margin. This misstatement is definitely material because the decisions of a financial statement user will be affected. The balance sheet testing did not identify this misstatement. The auditors will want to review or perform year-end revenue reconciliation between the production system and the general ledger posting. When the $3,000 cannot be substantiated, the auditors will add a reversal to the list of audit adjustments.

What does this all mean? The auditors will propose audit adjustments to the financial statements that management can accept and record or they can challenge. This is the time when management and auditors negotiate about the materiality of an entry and what that means. When the auditors and management agree to the adjustments, management will revise the financial statements and the auditors will issue a "clean," unqualified opinion. If management refuses to make the adjustments, the auditors can give the financial statements a qualified opinion, which means that they may not materially reflect the results of operations, refrain from issuing an opinion, or resign from the engagement.

An accountant goes into a pet shop to buy a parrot. The shop owner shows him three identical parrots on a perch and says, "The parrot on the left costs $500." "Why does that parrot cost so much?" asks the accountant. "Well," replies the owner, "it knows how to do complex audits."

"How much does the middle parrot cost?" asks the accountant. "That one costs $1,000 because it can do everything the first one can do plus it knows how to prepare financial forecasts."

The startled accountant asks about the third parrot, to be told it costs $4,000. Needless to say, this begs the question, "What can it do?"

To which the owner replies, "To be honest, I've never seen him do a darn thing, but the other two call him Senior Partner."[98]

Internal Audit Defined

Internal audit is an independent, objective assurance and consulting activity designed to add value and improve the company's operations. The New York Stock Exchange, or the NASDAQ, requires listed companies to have an internal audit function. The internal audit function can be developed in-house by hiring competent staff, or it can be outsourced. While outsourcing the internal audit function may be a cost-effective compliance solution for a company, the true benefit of the internal audit is lost. An outsourced internal audit function becomes an extension of the external auditors.

In the past, internal audit became known as the eyes and ears of management, but today an effective internal audit function is in partnership with all of the company stakeholders. Internal audits can assess the adequacy of and compliance with company policy, laws and regulations, and the effectiveness of operational activities. If you are lucky, your company has an established Internal Audit department. It is in the best interest of information technology to leverage the skills of internal auditors whenever possible. Competent internal auditors can be valuable resources for project teams, software implementations, and process structures and will welcome the opportunity.

The size and structure of the Internal Audit department is dependent on the needs of the company. A well-implemented Internal Audit department will be independent from all other departments. An effective Internal Audit department must be independent from all internal processes. The head of the department will report directly to the chairman of the audit committee, with dotted-line administrative reporting to the CFO.

The audit committee is a subset of the board of directors. The members of the audit committee must be independent board members with no other affiliation with the company. The company must disclose that one member of the audit committee is a financial expert, as required by Sarbanes-Oxley Act (SOX). The Securities Exchange Commission (SEC) defines a financial expert as one who understands GAAP and can assess the application of accounting principles; has experience preparing, auditing, analyzing, or evaluating financial statements; understands internal controls and procedures for financial reporting; and understands the audit committee oversight responsibilities. The responsibilities are to discuss with management, auditors, and stakeholders the adequacy of the internal controls system and risk management process, hold regular meetings with the director of internal audit, review significant findings and unsatisfactory internal audit reports.

The director of internal audit will hire competent staff to meet the unique needs of the company. While internal auditors are generally thought of as accountants, auditors can come from a variety of skill sets. Valuable skills for internal auditors include but are not limited to health care, engineering, environmental science, legal, compliance, risk management, security, and information technology.

The internal audit profession has standard-setting institutes and professional designations. The two most notable standard setters are the Institute of Internal Auditors (IIA) and the Information Systems Audit and Control Association (ISACA).

The IIA is a non-profit international professional association that was established in 1941. The primary mission is to provide leadership, promote the value of internal audit, and support professional development and education. The IIA published a comprehensive set of standards in October 2008. The International Standards for the Professional Practice of Internal Auditing (Standards) set forth basic principles that represent the practice of internal auditing. The Standards provide a framework for performing and promoting value-added internal auditing, establish a basis for evaluating internal audit performance, and foster improved company processes and operations.

The IIA offers a variety of professional designations. The premier designation is the Certified Internal Auditor (CIA),[101] which is the only globally accepted certification for internal auditors. To earn the designation, individuals demonstrate their competency by passing a comprehensive exam and adherence to a code of professional ethics. The CIA demonstrates professional knowledge of the internal audit profession and performs audits in accordance with the Standards.

ISACA is an independent, non-profit association that has been around since 1967. Initially incorporated as the EDP Auditors Association, ISACA has grown to serve a diverse global membership that drives development, adoption, and use of globally accepted practices for information systems. ISACA strives to be a one-stop shop for knowledge and value of information technology governance and controls.[102]

ISACA developed the only business framework for governance and management of enterprise-wide IT. Control objectives for information and related technology, also known as Control Objectives for IT (COBIT),[103] is an international set of generally accepted information technology controls and includes a set of generic processes that define process inputs and outputs, process activities, objectives, and performance measurements. COBIT links business goals to IT goals and provides metrics and maturity models to measure achievement. COBIT has become the most adopted framework by companies for SOX compliance.

The ISACA premier professional designation is the Certified Information Systems Auditor (CISA)[104] and is highly sought after by companies. The CISA designation requires passing rigorous exams and adherence to a code of professional ethics. The CISA designation is recognition of expert knowledge in the fields of IT security, IT audit, IT risk management, and governance.

Internal Audits

A well-designed Internal Audit department has a pervasive impact on the company because of the variety of tasks that are performed. These tasks include, but are not limited to, risk assessments, process reviews and audits to assess efficiency and identify control points, fraud investigations, testing of manual and automated controls, continuous controls monitoring, advising on project teams, and liaising with the external audit teams. External auditors have the option of relying on the work of a competent internal audit team. When the external auditors use a reliance approach, audit fees are generally reduced.

Internal audits are performed on processes at every level of the organization. The primary objective is to evaluate the efficiency of the process, identify controls, and test the effectiveness of existing controls. A process audit will include reviewing any policy and procedure documentation to ensure that it is complete and up to date, interviewing and observing personnel who perform the process to validate the documentation, identifying control points and procedures on any ERP systems that support the process.

Testing controls is a two-step process. Controls are evaluated for design efficiency and operational effectiveness. Evaluating a controls design consists of procedures to ensure that the control is mitigating the risks identified during the risk assessment process. Identified deficiencies in the design of a control generally result in no further testing. The need for the control is re-evaluated and remediation efforts begin to redesign the control. Testing a control for operational effectiveness is to ensure that the control procedures are followed. Deficiencies identified in the operational effectiveness of a control results in remediation efforts to ensure that the control activities are followed or the control is redesigned appropriately.

Since most operational processes are supported by information technology, IT audits are performed to evaluate the system's internal controls design and effectiveness, including efficiency and security protocols, development processes, and IT governance or oversight. IT auditing considers the potential risks and controls in information systems. Audit procedures and testing are developed to validate the operational efficiency of the controls for operations, data, integrity, software applications, security, privacy, budgets and expenditures, cost control, and productivity.

IT audits can be categorized as follows:

- Systems and applications audits verify that the systems and applications are appropriate, efficient, and controlled to ensure valid, reliable, timely, and secure input, processing, and output.

- Information processing verifies efficient processing by applications under normal and disruptive circumstances.

- System development verifies that the system development life cycle is used to ensure the project is meeting the objectives of the company.

- Management of the IT architecture verifies that the IT department organizational structure is appropriate and procedures exist to support good IT governance.

- Client/server intranets and extranets validate communications between the company and customers or vendors; among system applications; among employees; and between divisions is available and secure.

Systems Development Life Cycle

If you are lucky enough to have an Internal Audit department (stop laughing) or access to your Accounting department, you can leverage their expertise to make your life easier. Involving the internal auditor and accounting personnel in the early phases of the Systems Development Life Cycle (SDLC) can save a significant amount of time during implementation, can facilitate approvals from the project, stakeholders and provides a greater overall chance of project success.

The resources in every company are scarce. Here are some good ways to leverage the expertise of these internal resources:

- Planning — What regulations do we have to comply with?
- Analysis — Will this project cause regulatory or accounting troubles?
- Design — Where should the most effective control points be designed?
- Implementation — Auditors and accountants make great application testers.

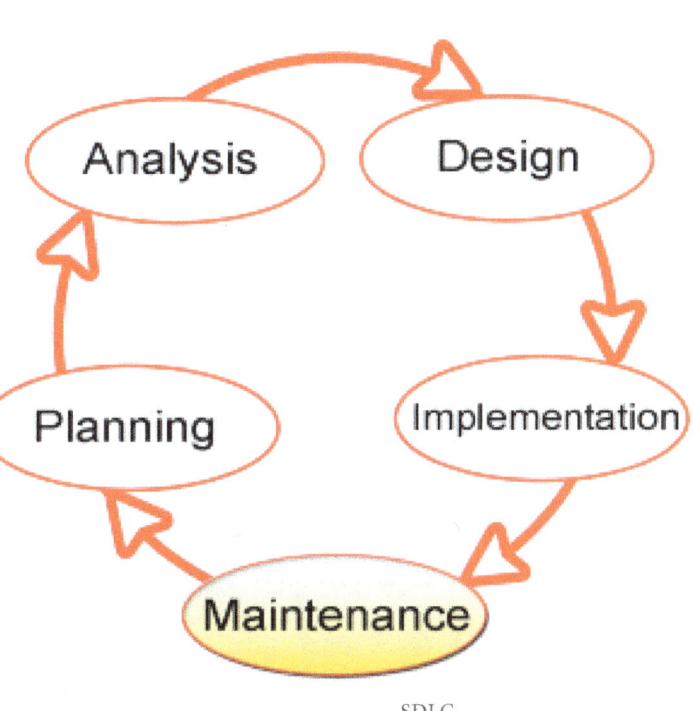

SDLC

What's the worst thing a group of internal auditors can do?
Go to the IT department and gang-audit the engineers.

CHAPTER 13

- FRIGGIN' BEAN COUNTERS - CONTROL THIS!

(2) Every issuer which has a class of securities registered pursuant to section 78l of this title and every issuer which is required to file reports pursuant to section 78o(d) of this title shall--

(B) devise and maintain a system of internal accounting controls sufficient to provide reasonable assurances that--

(i) transactions are executed in accordance with management's general or specific authorization;

(ii) transactions are recorded as necessary (I) to permit preparation of financial statements in conformity with generally accepted accounting principles or any other criteria applicable to such statements, and (II) to maintain accountability for assets;

(iii) access to assets is permitted only in accordance with management's general or specific authorization; and

(iv) the recorded accountability for assets is compared with the existing assets at reasonable intervals and appropriate action is taken with respect to any differences ~Foreign Corrupt Practices Act of 1977 [105]

Statement of Position (SOP) No. 29, issued by the American Institute of Certified Public Accountants (AICPA) in October 1958, requires auditors to consider internal controls as part of the financial statement audit. The thought was that the stronger the internal controls, the better the chance an error will be detected before the financial statements are made available to the public, which leads to less detailed testing the auditor would need to do and reduced audit fees. The Books and Records provision of the Foreign Corrupt Practices Act (FCPA) of 1977 was the first federal regulation that required businesses to devise and maintain reasonable internal accounting controls based on a recognized control framework. The best known control frameworks include:

- Committee of Sponsoring Organizations of the Treadway Commissions (COSO) Internal Control-Integrated Framework;
- Canadian Institute of Chartered Accountants (CICAs) Criteria of Control Framework (CoCo);
- The Basel Committee on Banking Supervision's Framework for Internal Control Systems;
- Control Objectives for Information and Related Technology (COBIT); and International Organization for Standardization (ISO).

Fast forward to the corporate accounting scandals involving Enron, Tyco, Adelphia, WorldCom, and Arthur Anderson, which led to Congress passing the

Sarbanes-Oxley Act (SOX) of 2002. Sections 404 and 302 are the provisions of SOX that require management's public statement that effective internal controls over financial reporting (ICFR) are in place and outline fines and penalties for not maintaining reasonable internal accounting controls.

Governance and controls are the primary conflict between the Accounting department and the rest of the company. Remember, the primary purpose of accounting is to use transactional data to provide meaningful information to decision makers. Internal controls are procedures or systems designed to mitigate identified risks; promote operational efficiency; ensure compliance with policy, procedures, and accurate financial reporting; safeguard assets; and help in reducing the potential for fraudulent behavior by management and staff. An effective system of internal controls helps ensure that the Accounting department is provided with data that is complete and accurate. Governance is the system of rules, practices, and processes that directs and controls the company.[106] It is often used synonymously with internal controls. The responsibility for governance and internal controls falls with management and the board of directors. Good governance sets the framework for achieving company goals and is the cornerstone for the success of a company. Good internal controls provide a mechanism to validate management assertions over financial reporting of existence, occurrence, valuation, allocation, rights, obligations, presentation, disclosure, and completeness.

Because of the significant number of accounting scandals, including Enron and WorldCom, over the past few years, governance and internal controls have become hot topics for legislative action. Companies are required to adopt a recognized control framework and management is required to certify annually, under the threat of personal fines and jail time, that the company's internal controls over financial reporting are adequate. This has caused the misconception that internal controls are accounting's problem and no other process in the organization has any impact on financial reporting. As previously stated, everything that occurs in a company affects Accounting; non-financial activities could cause situations that require disclosure in the financial statements in the form of contingent liabilities. A customer that slips and falls could initiate a lawsuit. A manufacturing plant that inadvertently discards hazardous material could cause an assessment of fines and clean-up costs that must be accrued and disclosed. The IT department that donates unwanted computers to a charitable organization without thoroughly cleaning the hard drives could disclose proprietary information or cause privacy breaches. The significance of any of these events could cause going-concern disclosures.

In 1992, the Committee of Sponsoring Organizations of the Treadway Commission (COSO)[107] established a common internal controls model that companies can use to assess their internal controls systems. The committee was sponsored and funded by five professional U.S. accounting associations and institutes: the American Institute of Certified Public Accountants (AICPA), the American Accounting Association(AAA),[109] the Financial Executives International (FEI),[110] the Institute of Internal Auditors (IIA),[111] and the Institute of Management Accountants (IMA).[112]

The COSO[113] model identifies five components of quality internal controls:

1. Control Environment – The foundation of effective internal controls that is defined by the attitude, awareness, and actions of management and directors commonly referred to as the "tone at the top." Managers and directors who believe an effective system of internal controls is critical to the success of the company will inspire the employees to embrace control activities as part of their normal job duties. The control environment includes documented policy and procedures, employee training and performance reviews, and a companywide code of conduct and ethics. The code of conduct documents management expectations for expected behavior and proper practices and outlines roles and responsibilities. An effective control environment has procedures in place for strategic planning and budgeting, which leads to goals and objectives that move the company in a common direction.

2. Risk Assessment - A systematic process of evaluating potential threats to the achievement of company goals and objectives. A risk is any undesirable event that hinders the company from achieving its goals and objectives. Different activities within a company could have very different risks, or a risk could span multiple activities. Risks should be categorized to ensure that all activities within a company are considered. There is no one-size-fits-all approach to identifying risks. Each risk assessment will be as unique as the company. Some example categories of risk are below.

   - Entity or organizational:
     - ▲ Governance - Rules, practices, and processes are out of date or do not exist.
     - ▲ People - The labor pool in a strategic geographical area is maturing to retirement.
   - Strategic - The IT infrastructure does not support the planned growth.
   - Operational - The assembly line breaks down and the parts for repair are obsolete.
   - Regulatory:
     - ▲ Compliance – Regulations exist the company does not know about.

- ▲ New - Regulations make the current strategy impractical.
- ● Financial - Interest rates cause borrowing to be impractical.
- ● Fraud - Key management personnel have outside interests that cause a conflict of interest.

Risks are evaluated in terms of likelihood and magnitude. The likelihood refers to the chance of the risk occurring, and the magnitude refers to the impact if the risk does occur. Impact is generally measured in financial terms, but it can also include undesirable impacts to the company's reputation, lost opportunities, or anything else that would prove meaningful to management. An agreed-upon value that represents high, medium, or low is assigned to the likelihood and magnitude for each identified risk. The product of the assigned values is the risk rating.

3. Information and Communication – Critical for executing strategic plans. Information is data that has been organized into a meaningful format. The value of information is measured in the benefit derived from it. Information is relevant when it leads to actions that will help a company achieve its goals and objectives. The only time information can lead to actions is when it is effectively communicated to those in a position to take action. Effective communication is accurate, timely, specific, and presented in a meaningful and relevant context. Formatting data into meaningful information and delivering effective communications are challenges that information technology has been instrumental in solving. The best-designed strategic plan will never be executed if it is not effectively communicated to the company's employees.

4. Control Activities - Procedures, techniques, and mechanisms to reduce the likelihood of a risk occurring and to mitigate the magnitude if the risk does occur. Control activities are implemented for specific reasons, such as mitigating the risks that could cause inefficient and ineffective operations or erroneous or fraudulent financial reporting. Control activities also help ensure that the company policies are followed and the policies comply with laws and regulations. All controls should be implemented based on a cost/benefit analysis. For example, it would not be cost-effective for IT to install software costing $10,000 that mitigates a risk that has a magnitude of $10.

Controls exist at every level of the company:

- ● Entity-level controls are environment controls to ensure good governance, such as documented policies and procedures;

- Operational controls are designed to ensure efficient and effective operations, such as user access and balance sheet reconciliations;
- Process controls are designed to ensure that management procedures are followed, such as quality assurance (QA) of patches before being installed; and
- Transaction-level controls are designed to ensure that each transaction complies with policies and any regulations, such as all refunds to customers are approved.

Controls activities are preventive or detective. Preventive control activities are designed to deter or prevent the occurrence of an undesirable event, such as error checking to ensure that all general ledger accounts are active before posting the batch. Detective control activities are designed to identify or detect undesirable events that have already occurred. Preventive controls are stronger controls than detective controls, because preventing an undesirable event is more efficient and cost effective than having to deal with the event after it occurred.

Control activities include but are not limited to:

1. Segregation (separation) of duties (SOD) – Separating transaction initiation, authorization, custody of assets, and record-keeping roles to deter fraud or mitigate potential errors. Proper SOD is one of the strongest, most cost-effective controls a company can implement.

2. Authorization – Review and approval of transactions by the appropriate level of management. In this context, a transaction includes any action affecting the business.

3. Records retention – Maintaining documentation to support transactions and compliance with any regulatory requirements in accordance with the required timeframe based on regulatory requirements or best practices.

4. Supervising and monitoring of operations – Observation or review of ongoing operational activity.

5. Physical safeguards – Physical access is restricted and cameras are implemented to protect assets.

6. Top-level reviews – Actual financial and operational results are compared to budgets, goals and objectives, and key performance indicators (KPIs) on a periodic basis.

7. Fraud prevention - Companywide fraud awareness and prevention training for all employees.

8. IT application controls - System controls over information processing, such as data validation, numerical sequences, and control totals. Application control examples include:

    - Completeness checks - All records were completely processed and support the completeness assertion.

    - Validity checks - Data that are input or processed are valid and support the occurrence assertion.

    - Authentication - All user identities were verified within the application system and support all management assertions.

    - Authorization - Only approved business users have access to the application system and support all management assertions.

    - Input controls - Data integrity is maintained through the user interface and supports all management assertions.

9. IT general controls (ITGCs) – or general computer controls, refers to the computer-based environment where application systems are developed, maintained, and operated. The objectives of ITGCs are to ensure that applications, and the integrity of programs, data files, and computer operations are properly developed and implemented. The most common ITGCs are:

    - Logical access controls over infrastructure, applications, anddata.
    - System development life cycle (SDLC) controls.
    - Program change management controls.
    - Data center physical security controls.
    - System and data backup and recovery controls.
    - Computer operation controls.

5. Monitoring - Processes to assess the design and operational effectiveness of internal controls. Monitoring itself is considered a control activity and is the regular assessment of the design and operating effectiveness of control activities. Internal Audit departments play a significant role in monitoring. As with any control activity, establishing monitoring procedures is also considered on a cost/benefit basis.

Management is responsible for establishing, enforcing, and evaluating internal controls activities. Controls activities can be manual or automated processes or procedures. Not all controls are created equal and have a specific hierarchy, with entity-level controls being the most important. Entity-level controls support the control environment. If the control environment activities prove to be effective, then testing and audit procedures can be reduced at all other levels. Typical control environment activities include a code of conduct and ethical behavior that is periodically presented to the employees; personnel policies and job descriptions; and the existence of board of directors and audit committee and other charters, such as the disclosure committee and compensation committee. A comprehensive anti-fraud training program and policy is a powerful tool for the control environment; it establishes a culture of zero tolerance for inappropriate behavior.

When internal or external auditors test the control environment, validating the existence of these documents is not enough. They must be comprehensive and up-to-date. The board of directors and the various committees must meet at regular intervals, and the meetings must be memorialized in the form of minutes. A great entity-level control is quarterly meetings of the audit committee to review the financial reporting package prior to public release. The organizational structure and attitudes of the CEO and CFO can also be powerful control environment activities.

After the control environment, the next set of important controls is the information technology general controls (ITGC) and any fraud prevention controls. Fraud is defined as any wrongful or criminal deception intended to result in any type of personal gain. Fraud prevention controls should be pervasive; that is, they should exist at every level and for every process of the company. Efficient internal controls provide reasonable assurance that the company will meet its goals and objectives. However, no system of internal controls can prevent collusion or management override. Collusion is two or more individuals who have agreed to act in secret or illegal cooperation to cheat and/or deceive. Management override of a control activity is a deliberate decision by management not to perform that control activity. Well-designed and implemented fraud prevention controls provide high visibility to any instance of inappropriate behavior that may occur.

There are several reasons that support the importance of IT controls as an addition to a company's fraud prevention and detection programs. Best practices insist that the many high-profile fraud prevention controls that are supported by information technology should be implemented. Examples include background checks as a condition of employment for new hires, subscribing to positive pay banking services to deter and detect the theft of accounts payable checks, and cameras located in inventory storage facilities. Examples of management override of these controls would be to hire someone who did not pass the background check, not submitting a list of accounts payable checks to the bank for positive pay monitoring, or turning off the security cameras.

The IT systems and support are one of the most significant investments a company will make in terms of money spent and resources allocated. A well-designed and managed IT system can give the company a competitive advantage by speeding up the development of new products, services, and business models; storing customer and supplier information; and providing information for improved decision making. Without a well-managed, robust information technology department, today's global organizations would not be effective.

ITGCs can be manual or automated. Automated controls are supported by an information system action or process, such as audit trail logs or validation error messages. Manual controls are supported by documentation, for example, requiring appropriate levels of management and stakeholders to review and sign off on the systems development life cycle (SDLC) project plan.

Logical access controls support the identification, authorization, and authentication of user activity within the information technology resources. The most common logical access controls are role-based security rules and user passwords. Role-based security is a powerful control because it builds in and enforces segregation or separation of duties (SOD). Password authentication ensures that only authorized individuals have access to the company's most valuable resources.

SDLC controls apply to a phased-in approach for planning, creating, testing, and deploying new technologies and enhancements to existing technologies. The SDLC applies to both hardware and software implementations. A well-developed and documented SDLC plan ensures that cooperation among the steering committee and overall project/program management, training, and quality assurance, are achieved for production acceptance of any major release. Documentation can include detailed workflows and process maps, committee presentations, and evidence that the project conforms to existing policies.

Program change management controls assure that any negative impacts of changes to the IT systems are minimized by using standardized processes for development, testing, and implementation. A robust quality assurance (QA) function is an essential component of change management, because it ensures that all changes to the IT environment are authorized, work as expected, and meet stakeholders' requirements.

Data center physical security controls apply to individuals being able to access the same room in which company data is stored. Data stored could include employee and customer protected information; vendor information and pricing contracts; and company proprietary information, including potential new products, project information, and financial information that is not available to the public. In an effort to save costs, many companies are outsourcing data center operations and other significant IT services to third parties. Outsourced relationships generate transactions that are reported in the published financial statements. Using a third-party does not relieve management of their responsibility for controls activities, including protecting data. A third party service must be vetted and selected that aligns with the company's goals and objectives.

As with anything accounting-related, third-party service providers must provide information that is useful for decision makers. So, there are rules. The standard issued by the AICPA is called Reporting on Controls at a Service Organization, and it provides guidance for a uniform framework to report on functions that are outsourced. Regulations such as SOX require greater transparency and international consistency in financial reporting because of the growth in Software as a Service (SaaS) and cloud computing. A vendor service provider that is offering outsourcing solutions will have an independent audit done on the controls of their organizations. The end result of these audits is a report referred to as a *Service Organization Control (SOC)* 1, 2, or 3 that the service provider can submit to their clients. A SOC 1 report is a written evaluation based on suitable criteria relative to written management assertions. SOC 2 & 3 reports are based on the five attributes of Trust Services Principles, which are physical and logical security, system availability, processing integrity, confidentiality, and privacy. It is management's responsibility to review these reports, ensuring that the controls executed by the service organization align with the company's goals and objectives. Management is also responsible for either implementing any client controls that are required by the third party or accepting the risk of any undesirable events as a result of not implementing the controls. Such controls could include procedures for notification of terminated employees who had the authority to physically access the data center, reconciliations of production data to the general ledger, or ensuring that backup and restore procedures work as expected.

System and data backup and recovery controls are an interesting topic. Everyone agrees that backups are important, and there is broad agreement that backing up data is critical. What about the software systems? They are often overlooked in the backup strategy. The frequency and scope of a backup is generally decided based on the cost/benefit relationship. A full system backup is more costly to perform than a data-only backup. Generally, a data backup is done on a regular basis, which is sufficient for many companies, however, many companies overlook the importance of testing the restore. What about the recovery? Many companies find after a catastrophic event that the diligently performed nightly backups cannot be restored. Regular testing of the backup and the restore are a critical component of proper ITGCs.

System and data backup and recovery are a subset of the broader topic of disaster recovery planning. A comprehensive disaster recovery plan is critical, but often overlooked. A catastrophic event could occur at any time without warning. Global companies are especially susceptible. Major hardware or software failures and natural disasters are the first risk considered, but what about seizure by a foreign government? The disaster recovery plan should be a documented roadmap for continued processing of critical jobs in the event of a major event. The plan should be updated on a regular basis, communicated to staff, and practiced to ensure smooth transition to the disaster procedures.

Computer operation controls are designed to ensure that IT systems function consistently and as planned. Operational documentation is comprehensive and designates roles and responsibilities relating to system start-up; backup, emergency, and shutdown procedures; instructions for error message debugging; system and job status reporting; and network load balancing. Application-specific operations instructions are also included and should define input sources, data formatting, restart procedures, and data storage requirements.

The next important level of control activities is closely related to ITGCs. Application controls are specific to the software that is being used to process transactions. These controls are valuable to the accounting application and any production systems that interface with the accounting application. Application controls relate to the accuracy and validity of data input. Application controls can include fields that are restricted to certain data types; audit trail logs with date, time, and user IDs for every input; validation checks that make sure debits equal credits before posting; prevention of duplicate vendor or customer number creation; and sequential transaction numbering. Application access controls ensure that users are authorized and authenticated and have access to the minimum system functionality necessary to perform the required job tasks.

Operational controls are of lesser significance because a strong control environment and a robust set of ITGCs and application controls have the best chance of preventing fraud or errors. They are implemented by management to ensure that risks to operating plans are executed and monitored in accordance with management goals and objectives. Operational controls describe procedures for controlling and managing activities, processes, products, and services associated with the significant operational risks.

Operational controls should:

1. Mitigate potential negative impacts to the control environment;
2. Align with the company's legislative and regulatory compliance strategies;
3. Identify areas for continuous improvement; and
4. Identify areas where achievement of goals and objectives is at risk.

Types of operational controls include documented standard operating procedures, pre-approved standard contract language, checklists, departmental meetings, escalation procedures, clear lines of authority, and management walk-through procedures.

Accounting controls are operational controls that are primarily detective in nature and include the account reconciliations, journal entry approvals, and trial balance actual to budget variances. Accounting is a process within a company, just like any other operational process. Reliable and accurate financial reporting is no different than reliable and safe products. A company that demands excellence does so at every level of the company. The primary objective of the SOX requirement of internal control over financial reporting (ICFR) is to ensure that controls are in place that will prevent or detect a misstatement to the financial statements. If the operational controls over all other processes are not effective, accounting controls will not prevent a misstatement. The most robust accounting controls would not make a bit of difference to the financial reporting if the company has a weak control environment and an uncontrolled information technology department and systems. One of the most important concepts to understand about the financial statements is that if the balance sheet is correct, all other financial statements are correct. Account reconciliations are considered ICFR and are done to prove that the balance sheet accounts of the trial balance equal an independent supporting document. The cash accounts must reconcile to the bank statements, investment and note payable accounts are supported by broker or bank statements and amortization schedules, and the accounts payable and receivable balances are supported by their respective aging reports. The accounts receivable and payable aging reports are a detailed list of all the individual ledger accounts. Additional controls include reconciliation of the revenue accounts to the production systems, review and approval of all journal entries posted to the general ledger, budget to actual variance analysis, and reconciliation of physical inventory counts to the inventory and cost of goods sold general ledger accounts.

Internal and external auditors design test procedures and gather evidence to verify the effectiveness of the company's controls. Audits must provide sufficient competent evidence of control effectiveness and adhere to a common set of information criteria. The evidence must be relevant, timely, correct, and consistent to the process to be usable. Accuracy, completeness, and validity are attributes of the integrity of the evidence. To achieve sufficient competent evidence, the auditors may perform testing of any information systems that are generating audit evidence. These tests will determine the reliability of the evidence, validating that confidential evidence is in fact confidential and compliance efforts are effective.

Internal controls that are supported by information technology are far more reliable and cost effective than manual controls because they are set up one time and should always operate in the same manner. While many believe that internal controls are non-value-added work, a comprehensive, well-designed system of internal controls becomes a routine task that ensures that management's goals and objectives are being met.

Auditor#1: My Auditee is an angel
Auditor#2: You're lucky, mine's still alive[144]
MIKE JACKA
1AONLINE.THEIIA.ORG

CHAPTER 14

- FRIGGIN' BEAN COUNTERS -
WE ARE NOT GOING TO JAIL

{ *Neither are we* }

Government 'help' to business is just as disastrous as government persecution... the only way a government can be of service to national prosperity is by keeping its hands off.
~Ayn Rand, American novelist, philosopher, playwright, and screenwriter [115]

Laws too gentle are seldom obeyed; too severe, seldom executed.
~Benjamin Franklin, American author, politician, and inventor [116]

In our personal ambitions we are individualists. But in our seeking for economic and political progress as a nation, we all go up or else all go down as one people.
~ Franklin D. Roosevelt [117]

WE'RE WATCHING YOU

No matter where you are on the political spectrum, government regulation is a fact of life. Compliance with government regulations has a significant affect on both accounting and information technology. Of major concern for every company are the regulatory environments they operate in, the cost of regulatory compliance, and the consequences of noncompliance. Information systems have to provide evidence to show compliance, and accounting has to prepare the required reporting to demonstrate that the company is in compliance. The select regulations discussed here can have a significant impact on companies that do not comply. If a company is knowingly noncompliant, at a minimum a contingent liability that has to be disclosed and accrued could be triggered. Remember, a contingent liability is a potential financial obligation based on future events. If a monetary liability is probable, then an estimated amount must be accrued; if reasonably possible or remote, a footnote disclosure must be made in the reporting. In addition, failure to comply with any of these regulations could cause bad press, irreversible damage to the company reputation, severe financial penalties, and potential individual liabilities. Unfortunately, with anything governmental, there are limited resources to enforce these regulations, which is one small reason why financial statement fraud still occurs. Well-designed IT systems, solid accounting procedures and a strong corporate ethical "tone at the top" are the best practices to help ensure financial statement fraud does not occur.

Prior to the Securities Act of 1933, sale securities (stocks, bonds, etc.) were regulated exclusively by blue sky laws, state laws that regulate the offering and sale of stocks to protect the public from fraud. Many of these laws still exist and are enforceable today; however, Article I, Section 8, Clause 3 of the U.S. Constitution, called the Commerce Clause, gives Congress power "To regulate Commerce with foreign Nations, and among the several States, and with the Indian Tribes." When contradictions between state and federal laws are identified, the courts determine which laws stand.

Securities Act of 1933

The Securities Act of 1933[118] (aka, the 1933 Act, the Securities Act, the Truth in Securities Act, the Federal Securities Act, or the '33 Act - Pub. L. 73-22, 48 Stat. 74, codified at 15 U.S.C. § 77a et seq) requires companies with publicly traded stock to make information about the company, its financial position, and any other relevant information available to the public. The U.S. Congress enacted the Securities Act of 1933 because of the stock market crash of 1929. The 1933 Act was passed May 27, 1933, during the Great Depression, and was signed by President Franklin D. Roosevelt. It was the first major federal legislation to regulate the initial offer and sale of securities (stocks, bonds, etc.).

SCC ACT OF 1933

The 1933 Act requires that any offer or sale of securities across state lines be registered, unless an exemption from registration exists. It is based on a philosophy of disclosure. The goal of the law is to require issuers (companies) to fully disclose all material information that a reasonable person would need in order to make a decision about the potential investment. Every public filing done by a company that is publicly traded is done in compliance with this law.

The SEC does not bring actions on behalf of individual investors, but the 1933 Act allows individual investors to bring civil actions under several provisions. Violation of the 1933 Act can lead to civil liability for the company and security underwriters.

Securities Exchange Act of 1934

The Securities Exchange Act of 1934[119] (the Exchange Act, '34 Act, or 1934 Act - Pub.L. 73–291, 48 Stat. 881, codified at 15 U.S.C. § 78a et seq.) was passed by Congress on June 6, 1934, and signed by President Franklin D. Roosevelt. It is a law that established and gave the Securities and Exchange Commission (SEC) responsibility for enforcement of the securities laws. The

US SEC COMMISSION

1934 Act governs the secondary trading of securities (stocks, bonds, and debentures) in the U.S. The '34 Act is also the basis for the regulation of the financial markets. Investors are protected by the requirement that financial information is available and fraud is prohibited. The '34 Act establishes penalties for those that defraud investors as well as trading practices that take advantage of information not available to all investors (known as insider trading). The SEC can bring civil enforcement action and criminal action for violations of the '34 Act. The '34 Act provides investors with a right to bring private suit against market participants that have defrauded them.

Foreign Corrupt Practices Act of 1977

The Foreign Corrupt Practices Act of 1977[120] (FCPA - 15 U.S.C. § 78dd-1, et seq.) is a U.S. federal law passed by Congress on December 19, 1977, and signed by President Jimmy Carter. It has two main provisions, one that addresses accounting transparency requirements under the Securities Exchange Act of 1934 and one concerning bribery of foreign officials. The SEC and the U.S. Department of Justice are charged with enforcing the provisions of the FCPA.

BRIBES

The provisions are enforceable against U.S. businesses, foreign corporations trading securities in the U.S., American nationals, and U.S. citizens and residents that act in furtherance of a foreign corrupt practice, even if they are not physically in the U.S. The provisions are also enforced against the actions of foreign nationals if they are physically in the U.S. at the time of their corrupt conduct.

The anti-bribery provision makes it illegal to pay a foreign official for the purpose of obtaining or retaining business. The Act also applies to any other recipient if part of the bribe is ultimately attributable to a foreign official, candidate, or party. These payments include money and anything of value. The act makes a distinction between bribery and a facilitation payment, which may be permissible under certain circumstances. Facilitation payments are made to expedite performance of duties that the foreign official is already bound to perform. The term "foreign official" is broadly defined and can include any person who has a direct or indirect affiliation with a government or government agency. Employees of international organizations are considered foreign officials. Materiality is not considered when determining violations of this provision. Remember, materiality is considering the significance of an item when it is reported. An item is considered material when it would affect the decision of a reasonable user. Anything offered to a foreign official, no matter what the value, is considered a violation of this provision.

The FCPA also requires companies with securities listed in the United States to meet the accounting transparency requirement (see 15 U.S.C. § 78m) that is designed to work with the anti-bribery provision. Corporations are required to keep books and records that accurately and fairly reflect the company transactions and to establish and maintain an adequate system of internal accounting controls.

Enforcement actions of the FCPA provisions can be brought against companies as well as individuals. Penalties for violations of the anti-bribery provisions against individuals are as follows:

- Civil penalty up to $10,000.
- Criminal fine up to $250,000 and or imprisonment up to 5 years.
  - ▲ Under the Alternative Fines Act, the fine may be increased to twice the gross financial gain or loss resulting from the corrupt payment.
  - ▲ A criminal fine imposed on an individual cannot be paid directly or indirectly by the company on whose behalf the person acted.

Penalties for violations of anti-bribery provisions against companies are as follows:

- Civil penalty up to $10,000.
- Criminal fine up to $2 million.
- The Alternative Fines Act may increase the criminal fine to twice the gain or loss resulting from the corrupt payment.

Penalties for violations of the accounting transparency provision against individuals are as follows:

- Civil penalty up to $100,000.
- Criminal fine up to $5 million or twice the gain or loss caused by the violation, and or imprisonment up to 20 years.
  - ▲ Fines cannot be paid directly or indirectly by the company on whose behalf the person acted.

Penalties for violations of the accounting transparency provision against companies are as follows:

- Civil penalty up to $500,000.
- Criminal fine up to $25 million or twice the gain or loss caused by the violation.

Transparency International

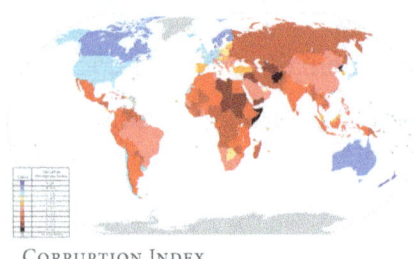
CORRUPTION INDEX

Many countries have passed regulations similar to the FCPA. As the global economy expands and IT projects expand into the global market, one resource to help with FCPA compliance is Transparency International (TI).[121] TI is a non-governmental coalition founded in May 1993 in Germany. The coalition does research, publishes reports, and compiles an annual Corruption Perception Index. TI defines corruption as abuse of power for private gain. The Corruption Perception Index is a comparative listing of corruption worldwide. Familiarity with this organization can benefit both businesses and investors. For example, if a company wishes to expand into unknown markets, this index will help with the strategy for developing those markets while complying with the FCPA.

Financial Services Modernization Act of 1999

MODERN BOARD ROOM

The Financial Services Modernization Act of 1999,[122] also known as the Gramm-Leach-Bliley Act (GLB - Pub. L. 106–102, 113 Stat. 1338), was passed November 12, 1999, and signed by President Bill Clinton. GLB repealed the Glass–Steagall Act of 1933. Glass-Seagull limited commercial bank securities activities and affiliations between commercial banks and securities firms. GLB allowed commercial banks, investment banks, and insurance companies to consolidate and create companies that are "too big to fail." The GLB defines financial institutions as companies that offer financial products or services such as loans, investments, and financial advice or insurance. GLB has two key rules with which both accounting and IT need to be concerned. The "financial privacy rule" governs the collection and disclosure of customers' personal financial information and extends to all companies that receive such information. The "safeguards rule" requires financial institutions to design, implement, and maintain safeguards to protect customer information. Since all customer information will reside in a database, securing that data from unauthorized access and disclosure will be the primary responsibility of the IT department.

Compliance with GLB is mandatory for all financial institutions, whether public or private, and the civil and criminal penalties for noncompliance are severe and can include fines and imprisonment. A financial institution can be subject to a civil penalty of not more than $100,000 for each violation. Officers and directors of the financial institution may be personally liable for civil penalties of not more than $10,000 for each violation. The financial institution and officers and directors can be subject to additional fines and imprisonment.

Sarbanes-Oxley Act of 2002

The Sarbanes-Oxley Act of 2002[123] (aka SOX, SOXA and SARBOX - Pub. L. 107–204, 116 Stat. 745) is known in the Senate as the Public Company Accounting Reform and Investor Protection Act and in the House of Representatives as the 'Corporate and Auditing Accountability and Responsibility Act.' The bill was passed July 30, 2002, by Congress and signed by President George W. Bush as a reaction to major corporate and accounting scandals, including Enron, Tyco International, Adelphia, Peregrine Systems, and WorldCom. These scandals cost investors, employees, and other stakeholders billions of dollars and adversely affected public confidence in the U.S. securities markets.

SOX

The bill includes 11 titles. The first, Title I, establishes the Public Company Accounting Oversight Board (PCAOB) to oversee the audits of public companies in order to protect the interests of investors and further the public interest in the preparation of informative, accurate, and independent audit reports. The PCAOB took over audit standard setting and oversight of public accounting firms from the AICPA. The bill also set standards for oversight of a public company's board of directors and management and increased the independence requirements of public accounting firms. Title II of SOX establishes standards for the external auditor's independence to limit conflicts of interest. Auditors must be independent in fact (real independence) and independent in appearance (perceived independence). This means that the auditors cannot have any financial or personal relationships with the company or the managers and directors who run the company. Title III mandates that executives take individual responsibility for the accuracy and completeness of the financial reports. Title IV establishes reporting requirements for all transactions, including off-balance sheet, pro forma, and company stock transactions executed by the corporate officers. Title IV also requires financial reports and disclosures on the effectiveness of internal controls. Titles V – VII have requirements for stock analysts and disclosure of conflicts of interests and define SEC authority and reporting requirements. Titles VIII – XI describe criminal penalties for manipulation or alteration and destruction of financial records and sentencing guidelines. The CEO is required to personally sign the corporate tax return and establish controls and procedures to identify corporate fraud.

There are two significant sections of SOX that have caused dissent in the corporate environment, Sections 302 from Title III and 404 from Title IV. Section 302 requires the CEO and CFO to certify that the financial reports were reviewed and do not contain any materially untrue statements or omissions and that the financial statements are fairly presented. Section 404 of Title IV sets forth that the signing officers are responsible for and have evaluated internal controls within the previous 90 days of the financial statements and have disclosed any significant changes in the control activities, and that a list of fraud and internal control deficiencies has been disclosed. Penalties for failure to certify the financial statements can include criminal penalties for the CEO and CFO individually. Many companies have a sub-certification process which requires all of the top executives to certify the financial statements.

Section 404 of Title IV has the greatest affect on IT. As we have previously stated, ITGCs and application controls are among the best controls a company can implement. Compliance with Section 404 requires a year-end assessment of the effectiveness of internal controls over financial reports that the CEO and CFO are certifying and on which the external auditors are reporting.

Health Insurance Portability and Accountability Act of 1996

HEALTHCARE

There are two significant health care laws that significantly affect information technology, and noted violations of these laws can create accounting issues. Violations can cause significant disclosures, such as contingent liabilities and going-concern issues, depending on the amount of fines, penalties assessed, and lawsuits started. The Health Insurance Portability and Accountability Act of 1996[124] (HIPAA - Pub.L. 104–191, 110 Stat. 1936) was passed by Congress on August 21, 1996, and signed by President Bill Clinton. HIPAA has two titles that significantly impact companies. Title I allows employees the option of maintaining employer health coverage at their expense. Title II has a significant impact on IT because it requires national standards for electronic health care transactions. The rules focus on protected health information (PHI) and electronic PHI (ePHI) gathered during the health care process and includes all health-related information. The Title requires the standardization of electronic transactions, code sets, and identifiers. Privacy and security rules are detailed. Any company that collects any type of health-related information is responsible for complying with HIPAA. Failure to comply can result in civil and criminal penalties that can be applied to companies and individuals.

Health Information Technology for Economic and Clinical Health Act of 2009

The Health Information Technology for Economic and Clinical Health Act[125], abbreviated HITECH Act, was enacted under Title XIII of the American Recovery and Reinvestment Act of 2009 (Pub.L. 111–5), signed by President Barack Obama. Under HITECH, the U.S. Department of Health and Human Services is spending $25.9 billion to promote and expand the adoption of health information technology. The primary challenge for IT professionals here is the fact that healthcare systems will have to interface and communicate while the privacy required by HIPAA is maintained.

The Bank Secrecy Act of 1970 and the U.S. Patriot Act of 2001

There are two significant laws targeting money laundering activities. Money laundering is an attempt to conceal the source of money obtained illegally. Illegally obtained money is stolen or proceeds from the sale of illegal drugs or stolen items. With the support of information technology, transactions that qualify for reporting can be easily identified. Violations of anti-money-laundering legislation can have significant effect on the financial health of a company. If violations are found, there can be large fines, and penalties for both the company and the individuals involved. These violations can also cause going-concern issues because of reputational harm and cash-flow issues.

Money Laundering

The Bank Secrecy Act (BSA)[126] was passed into law by the U.S. Congress and signed by President Richard Nixon in 1970. BSA is also referred to as the anti-money-laundering law (AML), or the BSA/AML. Banks and other financial institutions are required to report certain transactions to government agencies without notifying the customers that the reports were filed. Transactions subject to report are cash deposits or withdrawals of more than $10,000 in one day or the purchase of monetary instruments (money orders, cashier's checks, and traveler's checks) worth more than $3,000. The Currency Transaction Report (CTR) is filed with the Internal Revenue Service (IRS) and includes information about the person doing the transaction, such as address and occupation. There are heavy penalties for individuals and institutions that fail to file the appropriate information. There are also penalties assessed to banks that disclose to the customer that a report has been filed.

The U.S. Patriot Act (Public Law 107–56)[127] was passed soon after the September 11, 2001, terrorist attacks that occurred within the U.S. The Act was signed by President George W. Bush and expands the authority of U.S. law enforcement agencies to fight terrorist acts in the U.S. and abroad. The provision, called the Financial Anti-Terrorism Act, works with the Bank Secrecy Act. The Act grants governments the ability to control, monitor, and punish financial crimes and requires all financial institutions to implement anti-money-laundering programs.

U.S. Patriot Act

Payment Card Industry Data Security Standards (PCIDSS)

Credit Card Theft

The payment card industry (PCI) refers to various forms of electronic payment methods, such as credit and debit cards, automated teller machines (ATM), and point-of-sale (POS) transactions. On September 7, 2006, American Express, Discover, JCB, MasterCard Worldwide, and Visa International formed an independent council called the Payment Card Industry Security Standards Council.[128] The primary purpose of the council was to set standards for increasing controls around cardholder data to reduce credit card fraud. The PCIDSS are 12 requirements that businesses use to assess their own payment-card security policies and procedures. For a company to be PCIDSS compliant, the IT systems must be maintained to a stated set of security standards. A company that does not comply with PCIDSS can be significantly affected by fines, penalties, loss of electronic payment acceptance, and negative disclosures on the financial statements if the company is the victim of a security breach. A periodic self-assessment must be performed and submitted to the standards Council. A business that is compliant with PCIDSS receives a compliance certification and listing on the Council website.

Control Objectives[129]	PCIDSS Requirements
Build and Maintain a Secure Network	1. Install and maintain a firewall configuration to protect cardholder data
	2. Do not use vendor-supplied defaults for system passwords and other security parameters

Protect Cardholder Data	3. Protect stored cardholder data
	4. Encrypt transmission of cardholder data across open, public networks
Maintain a Vulnerability Management Program	5. Use and regularly update anti-virus software on all systems commonly affected by malware
	6. Develop and maintain secure systems and applications
Implement Strong Access Control Measures	7. Restrict access to cardholder data by business need-to-know
	8. Assign a unique ID to each person with computer access
	9. Restrict physical access to cardholder data
Regularly Monitor and Test Networks	10. Track and monitor all access to network resources and cardholder data
	11. Regularly test security systems and processes
Maintain an Information Security Policy	12. Maintain a policy that addresses information security

PCIDSS REQUIREMENTS

A theft of credit card data can create significant liability for a company. The Nevada legislature incorporated compliance to PCIDSS into state law, providing compliant businesses with protection from liability. Given this trend, a company would be proactive by implementing these standards.

Office of Foreign Asset Control (OFAC)

DEPARTMENT OF THE TREASURY

If the changing laws are not enough to worry about, there are also agencies that have been granted the authority to regulate business activity. One such agency that is extremely important and often overlooked is the Office of Foreign Asset Control (OFAC) of the U.S. Department of Treasury.[130] OFAC administers and enforces economic and trade sanctions based on U.S. foreign policy and national security goals against targeted individuals and countries engaged in terrorism, international narcotics trafficking, proliferation of weapons of mass destruction, and other threats against the U.S.

economy, national security, or foreign policy.[131] OFAC uses asset blocking and trade restrictions to accomplish foreign policy and national security goals. OFAC acts under the national emergency powers granted to the President and other specific legislation such as the Trading with the Enemy Act, passed by Congress in 1917 and signed by President Franklin D. Roosevelt. It allows for restriction of trade with countries hostile to the U.S.

OFAC acts to prevent trade, financial transactions, and other dealings called "prohibited transactions" between U.S. persons and companies with any individuals and organizations on the Specially Designated Nationals (SDN) list. The SDN is an OFAC publication that lists individuals and companies owned, controlled, or acting on behalf of targeted countries. The SDN also includes non-country-specific individuals, groups, and entities that have been linked to terrorism and narcotics trafficking. OFAC has the authority to grant exemptions to the prohibitions by either issuing a general license for certain transaction categories or by specific licenses issued on a case-by-case basis. Violation of OFAC sanctions can result in significant civil monetary penalties.

European Union Data Protection Directive of 1981 and Personal Information Protection and Electronic Documents Act of 1983

The company that operates globally must be aware that similar laws, rules, standards, and directives exist outside the U.S., and any U.S. company doing business globally needs to understand and comply with the requirements in every jurisdiction they do business in. Two notable requirements worth mentioning here are The European Union Data Protection Directive (EUDPD)[132] and Personal Information Protection and Electronic Documents Act (PIPEDA).[133]

The EUDPD has extremely restrictive requirements on the personal data that can be collected and how it is used. There are significant restrictions on transporting that data outside the European Union and comprehensive notification requirements to individuals whose data is being collected and how it is being used.

Data Thief

The Personal Information Protection and Electronic Documents Act (PIPEDA) is a Canadian federal regulation that governs the collection, use, and disclosure of personally identifiable information in the course of commercial transactions. PIPEDA gives individuals the right to know why and how a company collects, uses, and discloses their data. Companies are required to obtain consent when they collect and use personal information. The law also reassures the European Union that Canadian privacy laws are adequate to protect personal information of European citizens.

Jumpstart Our Business Startups (JOBS) Act of 2012

The newest U.S. government regulation to affect business and accounting is the JOBS Act. The Act was intended to promote job creation and economic growth by improving access to the capital markets for emerging, high-growth companies. The Act requires the SEC to amend the registration regulations, making it easier for companies to offer an IPO, allowing private companies to raise "small" amounts of capital through crowdfunding, and giving the SEC unprecedented authority. How the SEC will use this authority remains to be seen.

Why Is This Important?

Why does an awareness of the regulatory environment matter? Sonny Otis recently engaged a project team to expand into online global sales with a new service that builds custom ergonomic office equipment for people with disabilities. In order to accomplish the sales goals, the website must collect normal customer information such as name, address, and payment information. The company also needs information related to medical conditions, so that the office equipment can be properly constructed. The website is masterfully built, but the project team was not familiar with any of these laws and the potential accounting effects.

The first week of website traffic was significant and resulted in a number of orders. As fulfillment began, the warehouse found out that certain foreign addresses could not be delivered to because the delivery company refused to pick up the items. The addresses are in countries included in the OFAC database. Some of the custom products used materials that are restricted in some countries. Sonny Otis made a "contribution" to get a waiver from the governments. When the website was hacked, it was discovered that credit card and health information was not encrypted.

In this one example, we have violated the FCPA, HIPAA, PCIDSS, and OFAC regulations. The money has been returned, meaning revenue is not recognized and a contingent liability is accrued for the civil monetary penalties that are sure to be assessed. As a final blow, Accounting pulled the plug on the website until further work and compliance efforts were completed. Every time new projects are contemplated, it does not hurt to have a representative from the Accounting department, and at a minimum the Legal department should review the project plan for potential compliance issues.

"If you think you are getting too much government, just be thankful you're not getting as much as you're paying for"

- *Will Rogers*[145]

CHAPTER 15

– FRIGGIN' BEAN COUNTERS – WRAP IT UP PLEASE

We are almost done. You should have noticed this book is not a SOX manual or a fraud book. No matter how interesting and relevant emerging trends are, it is really important to get back to basics, such as the intertwined evolution of accounting and technology, why accounting rules and standards are established, the repetitive nature of double-entry bookkeeping, the difference between bookkeeping and accounting, and the real purpose of internal controls and how IT resources are affected. The historical information outlined in this book is extremely relevant to current trends. The following is my hit-list of important concepts to remember while navigating the BS infested cubicles of the Accounting department:

1. No matter how far removed you believe the IT project to be from the financial statements, at some point the Accounting department will be relying on your project, either by using the data as a direct source of reporting or by using data from other systems that directly rely on the new technology.

2. Producing high-quality, reliable, and accurate financial reporting is just as important to the long-term success of a company as producing high-quality products and services.

3. Materiality should never be an excuse for not doing something right. Materiality is a GAAP constraint that refers to the importance or value of a transaction to the financial statements. If a transaction is not considered significant enough to influence the decision-making process of financial statement users, then that item is not considered material.

4. SOX does not prohibit business activity. It requires that controls be in place to ensure that financial statements are accurately presented in all material respects.

5. Every project team should have one knowledgeable accountant.

6. Control activities should be designed to mitigate specific risks based on the significance of the risk to the company's achievement of their goals and objectives.

7. All employees are responsible for control activities.

8. All control activities should be implemented based on a cost/benefit analysis. You would not want to spend millions of dollars to mitigate a risk that has a ten dollar impact.

9. Accounting is a process within a company, just like any other operational process.

10. The most robust accounting controls will not make a bit of difference to the financial reporting if the company has a weak control environment and uncontrolled information technology systems.

11. One of the most important concepts to understand about the financial statements is that if the balance sheet is correct and properly supported, all other financial statements are correct.
12. It is not possible to design a system of internal controls that will mitigate the risks of management override and collusion.
13. If it does not make good common sense, then possibly you need more information or it just isn't the right thing to do.
14. Everyone should not have access to everything.
15. People who are in approval roles should not have access to create or post transactions. If you see this, you should raise your concerns to internal audit.
16. Never make database posting for transactions that should be posted through the user interface.
17. Automate and integrate as much as possible.

We have discussed many accounting and auditing concepts in this book with the goal of convincing IT and project managers that a solid partnership with your Accounting department is the primary key to ensuring success as we move forward with a global economy. The strategy used to make a convincing argument was to provide context, detail, and explanations for much of the BS you may have experienced while attempting to navigate the cubicles within your Accounting department.

Many of the concepts we discussed are thrown about without context, making accounting the last department anyone wants to deal with. When a project is near completion, accounting and internal audit are asked to sign off on a go-live. That is absolutely the wrong time to engage accounting and will almost ensure project failure. When brought in at the end, accounting and audit could identify controls that were not included, so they will not sign-off. If they do sign-off, they probably have some sort of manual workaround figured out. If accounting and internal audit are included in all phases of the project, then the sign off is a non-issue and the project has a better chance of success.

We discussed internal controls and how the accounting controls are process-level controls that have little impact on the financial statements if the control environment is weak and the information technology has no controls. There are no controls that can stop collusion or management override, but a solid partnership between IT and Accounting will be a strong deterrent to fraudulent behavior.

Satyam Computers Limited

Despite the best efforts of legislators, regulators, standard-setters within the accounting community, professional organizations, committees, and joint initiatives, financial statement fraud is still occurring today. Financial statement fraud undermines the integrity of financial reporting and contributes to economic losses by eroding investor confidence. A significant case of corporate fraud committed by the chairman of Saytam Computer Services came to the public's attention in 2009. This case highlights the undesirable effects of management collusion at the highest levels with internal and external parties, management override of control activities, the impacts of a weak control environment, and uncontrolled IT resources.

As you read through this fraud case, keep in mind the following what-if scenarios:

1. What if the help desk understood segregation of duties and was able to raise awareness that the head of internal audit was granted access to create invoices and was able to raise awareness?

2. What if the project managers and implementation team understood the need to fully integrate the accounting application?

3. What if network security understood the importance of strong passwords in the accounting application?

4. What would the impacts have been fraud if whistleblower and audit controls detected fraud in the early stages?

Satyam Computers Limited, an India-based information technology consulting firm, was founded in 1992. The company quickly grew to serving customers in 66 countries with over 53,000 employees. Company stock was sold on the Bombay Stock Exchange (BSE), National Stock Exchange of India Ltd. (NSE), and the New York Stock Exchange (NYSE). Satyam began trading on the NYSE in 2001.

The NYSE and NASDAQ revised their Listed Company Rules to include governance. The revised requirements align with SOX and were approved by the SEC in November 2003. Since Satyam was listed on the NYSE in 2001, they were subject to all of the Listed Company Rules, which included compliance with SOX.

On January 7, 2009, Mr. Ramalinga Raju, the chairman of Satyam Computer Limited, disclosed in a letter to the board of directors that "he had been manipulating the company's accounting numbers for years." Mr. Raju claimed that he overstated assets on Satyam's balance sheet by $1.47 billion. His letter of confession stated that "he could just not handle any more" — money, power, success, and prestige compelled Mr. Raju to violate all of his fiduciary duties. According to India's Central Bureau of Investigation (CBI), the fraud began in 1999 when the company decided that double-digit annual growth was the primary objective. In December 2008, Satyam had a total market capitalization (aggregate valuation of the company based on the current share price and total number of outstanding stocks) of $3.2 billion USD. In spite of corporate governance, independent external audits and a whistleblower program, the fraud was not identified by any of the means that are considered good corporate governance. PriceWaterhouse Coppers (PwC), the audit firm, did not detect any of the defalcation; in fact some PwC auditors engaged by Satyam have been prosecuted as participants. Nearly $1.04 billion in bank loans and cash that the company claimed to own was non-existent. Satyam also underreported liabilities on its balance sheet and overstated income nearly every quarter over the course of several years in order to meet analyst expectations. According to reports, Raju and his brother, B. Rama Raju, the Managing Director, "hid the deception from the company's board, senior managers, and auditors." The case of Satyam's accounting fraud has been dubbed as "India's Enron."[134]

The Serious Fraud Investigation Office (SFIO) launched an investigation. The SFIO is a multidisciplinary organization that investigates serious financial frauds in India and is under the jurisdiction of the Indian government. The SFIO issued a report in April of 2009 that found the former management of Satyam kept loopholes in the Oracle Financials accounting software. The company's Oracle installation was deliberately made very complex for inflating profits. A complex set of systems was implemented to work outside of Oracle. Different departments of the company were not integrated electronically, and management overlooked this weakness, which resulted in the duping of investors and other stakeholders.[135]

No internal passwords were required to access the Oracle Financials database, which increased the possibility of unauthorized changes to the programs. At the application level, passwords were unsecured to facilitate the fraud. The invoice management system had weak password protection, making the system vulnerable to misuse, which allowed the director of internal audit to create fake invoices.[136]

Satyam used a complex billing system. The first application was used to bill project time and interface with the second system, called the Invoicing Management System (IMS). IMS would gather all of the information from Satyam's various project management systems to create the final invoice for the customer and interface with Oracle Financials. IMS was enabled to allow porting of data through Excel directly into the IMS databases. When Excel porting was done, there was no need complete the billing process as designed. To complete the Excel porting, an Admin ID and password were used to generate invoices directly from IMS. The Admin ID and password were shared with the entire accounts receivable team. Excel attachments with invoicing data was received by finance, imported to IMS, and then the invoice was hidden in the system, but the revenue was recorded.[137]

SFIO also found that to balance the cash collection against the fictitious invoices, receipts were forged in the current account maintained with the Bank of Baroda, the New York branch, and subsequently they were shown to be transferred to other bank accounts as fixed deposits. Raju created fake statements and forged quarterly balance confirmation letters to validate the amount of the fixed deposits and the interest accrued. These forged account statements and confirmation letters were fed into Oracle Financials for quarterly audits of the company. As the fraud grew, three other bank accounts in India, Citi Bank, HDFC Bank, and HSBC, were also used for the purpose of falsification of current account balances recorded to the general ledger.[138]

The SFIO report cites a serious control deficiency in the system that facilitated the entering of unauthorized transactions, making unauthorized payments, and non-detection of unauthorized activities. The report goes on to say that PwC, which audited Satyam's accounting software, had pointed out to the company's audit committee that this weakness in the system may result in misstatement of the annual or interim financial statements. The report further says that the audit committee chairman denied receiving such an input.[139]

Satyam had paid PwC twice the audit fee that would have been paid to other firms. Was PwC complicit in the crime? Satyam was accused of fraud on two separate occasions and the audit firm did not give the accusations any importance. While performing audit procedures, PwC did not follow proper established audit procedures for auditing bank accounts or accounts receivables. Confirming bank balances and accounts receivable is an audit test where the party is contacted by the auditor to validate that the balance is correct.[140]

In the aftermath of the fraud, Raju and his brother, the CFO, the head of internal audit, and several PwC auditors were arrested and charged with fraud. In July 2014, the SEBI ordered Raju and four former executives to repay $308 million in alleged gains and 12% annual interest from the time the fraud was found. Satyam was acquired through public auction by Tech Mahindra, an Indian multinational provider of information technology, networking technology solutions, and business support services to the telecommunications industry.

The Satyam scandal highlights how a solid partnership between IT and Accounting could have prevented much of the fraudulent activities by identifying the fraudulent activities earlier. At the same time highlighting how no system of controls can overcome management override and collusion. Although management override and collusion cannot be easily detected, you can design an environment to mitigate and reduce the impacts. Financial statement fraud does a significant amount of damage to economies, stock markets, and the lives of employees and customers. Maybe by creating a solid foundation of cooperation, we can stop the next big fraud from happening before more unnecessary regulation is passed.

About the Author

Karla has amassed a significant amount of experience over the past 15 years. She has worked in both Accounting and Audit departments and is currently consulting for both public and private companies. Working with all levels of employees and processes of an organization has given Karla a unique perspective on the issues surrounding organizations. She is both proactive and practical in her approach to accounting and compliance issues.

She is an active member of the AICPA and the IIA, where she served two terms as the chapter president for the San Fernando Valley chapter of the IIA. She earned her bachelor of science in Accounting from the University of Central Florida and her masters' of Information Technology Management from the Florida Institute of Technology.

INDEX

A

Account Sales Register · 90, 93

Accountancy · 43, 74

Accounting records · 26, 32, 78

Accounting software · 52, 98

Accounting Standards Board · 60

Accounts Payable (AP) · 15, 22, 73, 83, 90, 98, 99, 110, 119, 120, 133, 147, 154, 156, 173

Accounts Receivable (AR)   57, 58, 73, 83, 90, 95, 96, 100, 105, 108, 111, 114, 129, 138, 148, 153, 177

Activity Based Costing · 78

Actuarial accounting · 78

American Institute of Certified Public Accountants (AICPA) · 61, 167

American Association of Public Accountants · 43

American Institute of Accountants · 60

American Recovery and Reinvestment Act of 2009 · 188

Ancient Egypt · 25, 28 Annual budgets · 30

Apple · 51, 52

Arabic numerals · 14

Arithmometer · 41

Auditing · 43, 58, 61, 74, 78, 144, 153, 155, 161

Augusta Ada King, Countess of Lovelace · 42

Automatic Sequence Controlled Calculator (ASCC)   46

B

Babylon · 26, 55, 89

Bank Secrecy Act · 188

Bell Laboratories · 49

Blaise Pascal · 37

Bookkeeping · 8, 11, 16, 32, 33, 56, 57, 61, 65, 68, 74, 75, 85, 89, 93, 96, 97, 100, 118, 131, 154, 195

Budgeting · 22, 72, 84, 169

Business transactions · 56, 74, 77

C

Cash Basis · 77

Cash Book · 90

Cash Management · 72

Certified Public Accountant (CPA) · 43, 74, 167

Charles Babbage · 42, 46

Charles Xavier Thomas de Colmar · 41

Chart of Accounts · 89, 90, 95, 96, 101, 107, 111, 124, 143

Classical Greece · 28

Claude Elwood Shannon · 45

Clay tablets · 26

COBOL · 52

Codex accept et expense · 16

Corporation · 58

Cost Accounting · 42, 78

Cuneiform Script · 14, 26

D

Day Books · 29, 89

Debt Service · 72

Deeds of the Divine Augustus ·55

Differential Analyzer · 45

Differential Engine · 41

Doomsday Book · 31

Double-entry bookkeeping · 32, 56, 57, 89, 91, 92, 99, 100, 105, 148, 154, 195

Dr. J Prosper Eckert · 47

Dr. John Mauchly · 47

E

Eckert-Mauchly Computer Corporation (EMCC) · 48

Economic growth · 14, 25, 37, 61, 192

Edinburgh, Scotland · 27
Electronic Delay Storage Automatic Computer (EDSAC) · 48
Electronic Discrete Variable Automatic Computer (EDVAC) · 47
Electronic Numeric Integrator and Calculator (ENIAC) · 47, 51
Enron Corporation · 43, 58
European Union Data Protection Directive · 191

F

Father of information theory · 45
Finance · 56, 67, 71
Financial Accounting Standards Board (FASB) · 60, 62, 116
Financial statement manipulation · 141, 142
Foreign Corrupt Practices Act (FCPA) · 183, 203
FORTRAN · 52

G

Generally Accepted Accounting Procedures (GAAP) · 59, 77, 106, 117, 127, 131, 148, 161, 195
General Ledger · 73, 82, 91, 94, 99, 100, 105, 111, 115, 118, 124
Geoffrey W.A. Dummer · 50
Glasgow · 40
Gottfried Wilhelm Von Leibniz · 38
Great Roll of the Exchequer · 31

H

Health Insurance Portability and Accountability Act of 1996 (HIPAA) · 187
Herman Hollerith · 42, 100
Howard Hathaway Aiken · 46

I

Income Tax Basis 77
Industrial Revolution · 39
Institute of Accountants · 40

Integrated circuit · 41, 50

Intel 8080-MOS 6502 processors · 51

Internal Revenue Service (IRS) · 61, 65, 188

International Financial Reporting Standards (IFRS) · 61, 116, 156

International Business Machines (IBM) · 42, 46, 49, 51, 109

International Accounting Standards Board (IASB) · 62, 116

Interstate Hosiery Mills · 58

Intuit · 52

J

Jack St. Clair Kilby · 50

John Bardeen · 49

Journals · 89

Julius Edgar Lilienfeld · 49

K

King of England · 31

L

Ledger · 44, 56, 73, 82, 90, 95, 97

Leibniz wheel · 39, 41

Luca Pacioli · 56

M

McKesson & Robbins · 58

Medieval period · 30

Merchandise Bought Book · 77, 90

Merchandise Sold Book · 90, 94, 96

Mergers and Acquisitions (M&A) · 72

Mesopotamia · 25

Microprocessors · 51

Modified Cash Basis · 77

N

National Association of State Boards of Accountancy (NASBA) · 43

National Uniform CPA Exam · 43

O

Other Comprehensive Basis of Accounting (OCBOA) · 77

Office Foreign Asset Control (OFAC) · 169

P

Partnership · 65, 67, 160, 196

Payment Card Industry Data Security Standards (PCI-DSS) · 189

Payroll (PR) · 73, 90, 98, 111, 121

Peachtree · 52

Personal Information Protection and Electronic Documents Act (PIPEDA) · 191

Philco Transac S-1000 scientific computer · 49

Principles of Accountancy, American Bookkeeping Series · 74, 91, 153

Proctor & Gamble · 52

Production Accounting · 78

Publicly traded · 61, 65, 81, 144, 143, 182

Purchase · 107

Q

Queen Victoria · 40

R

Renaissance · 32, 56

Revenue · 50, 61, 66, 67, 72, 77, 83, 89, 97, 105, 108, 11

Robert Norton Noyce · 58

Royal Charter 26

S

S-2000 electronic data processing computer · 49

SAP AG · 52

Sarbanes-Oxley Act of 2002 (SOX) · 58, 155, 161, 168, 175, 177, 186

S-corporation · 66

Scott Cook · 52

Scribes · 27

Securities Exchange Commission (SEC) · 61, 129, 161, 182

Securities Exchange Act of 1934 · 182

Sexagesimal · 26

Siemens AG · 50

Sir Maurice Vincent Wilkes · 48

Social Accounting · 79

Sole proprietor · 66

Stakeholders · 67, 141, 160, 164, 174, 186, 198

Statutory Basis · 77

Sumeria · 26

T

Tabulating Machine Company · 42

Tom Prolix · 52

TRADIC · 49

Transistors · 33, 49, 50

Trial Balance · 57, 74, 90, 99, 105, 125

U

Ultramares Corporation v. Touche · 57

United States Tax Code · 66

UNIVersal Automated Computer (UNIVAC) · 48, 51

U.S. Census Bureau · 42, 48

V

Vacuum tube technology · 47

Vannevar Bush · 45

W

Walter Brattain · 49

Werner Jacobi · 50

William Bradford Shockley · 49

William the Conqueror · 30

ENDNOTES

1 Funny insults and put downs. Retrieved from http://www.the-alternative-accountant.com/index.html

2 Russian Proverb

3 - 4 Project proverbs. Retrieved from http://www.project-systems.co.nz/project-proverbs.html

5 Retrieved from http://www.brainyquote.com/quotes/quotes/c/confucius141560.html

6 Kagan, D., Ozment, S., & Turner, F. M. (1987). The western heritage. Location: Publisher.

7- 15 Alexander, J. R. (2002). History of accounting. New York: Association of Chartered Accountants in the United States. Retrieved from http://documents.clubexpress.com/documents.ashx?key=7ZPfhrgSH4ej5qOo06gTZ1j/WfzYw%2BhpXBNOQ%2BBbRiWgYV1UQpbPezRxbi/PDVo7X

16 Babbage, C. (1864). Passages from the life of a philosopher. Retrieved from https://archive.org/details/passagesfromlif01babbgoog

17 Blaise Pascal biography. Retrieved from http://www.biography.com/people/blaise-pascal-9434176

18 Cook, C. L. (1988). How computers have simplified accounting. Retrieved from http://www.yale.edu/ynhti/curriculum/units/1989/7/89.07.06.x.html

19 Look, B. C. (2014). Gottfried Wilhelm Leibniz. Retrieved from http://www.britannica.com/EBchecked/topic/335266/Gottfried-Wilhelm-Leibniz

20 Alexander, 2002 pages 12 - 13.

21 Charles Xavier Thomas de Colmar. Retrieved from http://www.britannica.com/EBchecked/topic/725533/Charles-Xavier-Thomas-de-Colmar

22 Key people – Charles Babbage. (2008). Retrieved from http://www.computerhistory.org/babbage/charlesbabbage/

23 Key people – Ada Lovelace. (2008). Retrieved from http://www.computerhistory.org/babbage/adalovelace/

24 Herman Hollerith. Retrieved from http://www.census.gov/history/www/census_then_now/notable_alumni/herman_hollerith.html

25 Punched card tabulating machines. Retrieved from http://www.officemuseum.com/data_processing_machines.htm

26 - 28 Alexander, 2002.

29 Miranti, P. J. (1996). Birth of a profession. Retrieved from http://www.nysscpa.org/cpajournal/1996/0496/features/f14.htm

30 About the AICPA. Retrieved from http://www.aicpa.org/About/Pages/About.aspx

31 Dennis, M. A. Vannevar Bush. Retrieved from http://www.britannica.com/EBchecked/topic/86116/Vannevar-Bush

32 Claude Shannon. Retrieved from http://www.nyu.edu/pages/linguistics/courses/v610003/shan.html

33 Howard Hathaway Aiken. Retrieved from http://www.britannica.com/EBchecked/topic/10473/Howard-Hathaway-Aiken

34 Encyclopedia of Information Technology, pg 600, Atlantic publisher & distributers

35 Milestone-proposal: Harvard Mark I computer, 1944 – 1959. Retrieved from http://www.ieeeghn.org/wiki6/index.php/Milestone-Proposal:Harvard_Mark_1_Computer,_1944_-_1959

36 J. Presper Eckert: 1990 computer entrepreneur award recipient. Retrieved from http://www.computer.org/portal/web/awards/entrepreneuereckert

37 Encyclopedia of Information Technology, Atlantic Publishers & Distributors, pg. 651

38 The electronic numerical integrator and computer (ENIAC). (2003). Retrieved from http://web.mit.edu/invent/iow/mauchly-eckert.html

39 Payne, M. (2010). History of computers – UNIVAC. Retrieved from http://wiki.sjs.org/wiki/index.php/History_of_Computers_-_UNIVAC

40 ENIAC, 2003.

41 Gregersen, E. (2013). Sir Maurice Vincent Wilkes. Retrieved from http://www.britannica.com/EBchecked/topic/725595/Sir-Maurice-Vincent-Wilkes

42 Transistors. Retrieved from http://transistors.askdefine.com/

43 Invention – The birth of the IC. Retrieved from http://www.integratedcircuithelp.com/invention.htm

44 The integrated circuit of Jack Kilby and Robert Noyce. Retrieved from http://history-computer.com/ModernComputer/Basis/IC.html

45 Jack Kilby biography. Retrieved from http://www.biography.com/people/jack-kilby-40499

46 Gordon E. Moore & Robert N. Noyce: 1978 Harry Goode memorial joint award recipients. Retrieved from http://www.computer.org/portal/web/awards/moore-goode

47 The history of computers. Retrieved from http://www.ptc.dcs.edu/Moody/comphistory/comphistory_print.html

48 Intel's first microprocessor. Retrieved from http://www.intel.com/content/www/us/en/history/museum-story-of-intel-4004.html

49 Singh, P. K. (2009). Basics of computer. New Delhi: V.K. (India) Enterprises.

50 About SAP AG. Retrieved from http://global.sap.com/corporate-en/index.epx

51 Dyer, B. (2004). Oral history interview. Retrieved from http://conservancy.umn.edu/handle/107274

52 InfoWorld, InfoWorld Media Group, Inc. Jun 11, 1979, page 22

53 Company fast facts. Retrieved from http://about.intuit.com/about_intuit/press_room/fast_facts/

54 Adopted for this work by Linwood Sasser

55 Retrieved from http://www.brainyquote.com/quotes/quotes/a/alberteins386089.html

56 Alexander, 2002.

57 The Mesopotamians. Retrieved from http://timerime.com/es/periodos/1561105/Hammurabi/

58 Alexander, 2002.

59 Alexander, 2002.

60 De Computis – A name rich in history. Retrieved from http://www.decomputis.com/about.htm

61 - 63 Alexander, 2002, page 9.

64 Facts about FASB. Retrieved from http://www.fasb.org/jsp/FASB/Page/LandingPage&cid=1175805317407

65 Selected staff accounting bulletins. Retrieved from http://www.sec.gov/interps/account.shtml

66 "Enron's Ken Lay: 'There's no other shoe to fall.'" (Aug 23, 2001). Bloomberg Businessweek. Retrieved from http://www.businessweek.com/stories/2001-08-23/enrons-ken-lay-theres-no-other-shoe-to-fall

67 https://www.facebook.com/ntjokes/posts/541946325835627

68 "What managers really do" (Aug 17, 2009). The Wall Street Journal. From an interview with MIT Sloan Management Review Senior Editor Martha E. Mangelsdorf in Aug, 2009 Retrieved from http://online.wsj.com/

69 Goodyear, L. E. (1913). Principles of accountancy: American Bookkeeping Series. Retrieved from http://www.archive.org/

70 Goodyear, 1913.

71 http://www.jokes.net/accountantvisitsthenaturalhistorymuseum.htm

72 Retrieved from http://www.brainyquote.com/quotes/authors/b/bernard_ebbers.html

73 Types of Accounting | Financial, Management, Public, Tax ... (n.d.). Retrieved from http://accounting-simplified.com/financial/types-of-accounting.html

74 Financial Accounting. Retrieved from http://www.investopedia.com/terms/f/financialaccounting.asp

75 Retrieved from http://www.worldofquotes.com/topic/Profession+and+professionals/1/index.html

76 http://www.thorstenconsulting.com/2FGA/JOKE.htm

77 Retrieved from http://www.brainyquote.com/quotes/quotes/a/alberteins383803.html

78 - 79 Goodyear, 1913.

80 Accounting cycle. Retrieved from http://www.investopedia.com/terms/a/accounting-cycle.asp

81 Analysing the importance of financial management. Retrieved from http://www.ukessays.com/essays/accounting/analysing-the-importance-of-financial-management-accounting-essay.php

82 http://www.lifehealthpro.com/2012/04/17/7-great-accountant-jokes?t=life-planning-strategies&page=8

83 12 accountants jokes. Retrieved from http://www.manwalksintoajoke.com/accountants

84 http://www.journalofaccountancy.com/Issues/2001/Jun/TheRightWayToRecognizeRevenue

85 IBM dictionary of computing (10th ed.). (1993). New York: McGraw-Hill.

86 Revenue recognition – Joint project of the FASB and IASB. Retrieved from http://www.fasb.org/revenue_recognition.shtml

87 http://www.the-alternative-accountant.com/accounting-jokes.html

88 State of the Union Addresses by John F. Kennedy. (1961). Retrieved from http://www.google.com/url?sa=t&rct=j&q=&esrc=s&frm=1&source=web&cd=7&cad=rja&uact=8&ved=0CE4QFjAG&url=http%3A%2F%2Fwww2.hn.psu.edu%2Ffaculty%2Fjmanis%2Fpoldocs%2Fuspressu%2FSUaddressJKennedy.pdf&ei=5sI4U9WhKsew2gW49oGgAQ&usg=AFQjCNFPUWRdscp_q_9d5_LwgAd6725lng&sig2=RaLjK7mIQwhH5n4lBXissQ

89 Asimov, A. (1981). Change! 71 glimpses of the future. Boston: Houghton Mifflin.

90 Plato. Phaedrus. Retrieved from http://classics.mit.edu/Plato/phaedrus.html

91 McDonald, C. L., & Noll, D. (1998). What are start-up costs and how should entities account for them? Journal of Accountancy. Retrieved from http://www.journalofaccountancy.com/Issues/1998/Jul/accapps.htm

92 One liner jokes about accountants. Retrieved from http://www.accountanttown.com/site/one-liner-jokes-about-accountants

93 Goodyear, 1913, page 72.

94 https://www.sec.gov/rules/final/33-7919.htm

95 Reports on audited financial statements. Retrieved from http://www.aicpa.org/Research/Standards/AuditAttest/DownloadableDocuments/AU-00508.pdf

96 Generally accepted auditing standards. Retrieved from http://www.aicpa.org/Research/Standards/AuditAttest/DownloadableDocuments/AU-00150.pdf

97 Auditing standard no. 15: Audit evidence. Retrieved from http://pcaobus.org/standards/auditing/pages/auditing_standard_15.aspx

98 http://www.merinews.com/humourCategory.jsp?HumourMethod=Popular&humourID=115

99 Retrieved from https://www.isaca.org/

100 International standards for the professional practice of internal auditing (standards). (2008). Retrieved from https://na.theiia.org/standards-guidance/Public%20Documents/IPPF%202013%20English.pdf

101 Why become certified? Retrieved from https://na.theiia.org/certification/new/pages/why-become-certified.aspx

102 About ISACA. Retrieved from http://www.isaca.org/about-isaca/Pages/default.aspx

103 COBIT 4.1: Framework for IT governance and control. Retrieved from http://www.isaca.org/Knowledge-Center/cobit/Pages/Overview.aspx

104 Certified Information Systems Auditor (CISA). Retrieved from http://www.isaca.org/Certification/CISA-Certified-Information-Systems-Auditor/Pages/default.aspx

105 The foreign corrupt practices act. Retrieved from http://www.justice.gov/criminal/fraud/fcpa/docs/fcpa-english.pdf

106 Corporate governance. Retrieved from http://www.investopedia.com/terms/c/corporategovernance.asp

107 Retrieved from http://www.coso.org/

108 Retrieved from http://www.aicpa.org/

109 Retrieved from http://aaahq.org/

110 Retrieved from http://www.financialexecutives.org/

111 Retrieved from https://na.theiia.org/

112 Retrieved from http://www.imanet.org/

113 Internal control – Integrated framework. Retrieved from http://www.coso.org/documents/coso_framework_body_v6.pdf

114 Service organization control (SOC) reports. Retrieved from http://www.aicpa.org/

115 Retrieved from http://www.brainyquote.com/quotes/quotes/a/aynrand124850.html

116 Poor Richard's Almanack. Retrieved from http://en.wikiquote.org/wiki/Poor_Richard's_Almanack#1756

117 "One third of a nation": FDR's second inaugural address. Retrieved from http://historymatters.gmu.edu/d/5105/

118 Retrieved from https://www.sec.gov/about/laws.shtml

119 Securities exchange act of 1934. Retrieved from https://www.sec.gov/about/laws/sea34.pdf

120 Foreign corrupt practices act. Retrieved from http://www.justice.gov/criminal/fraud/fcpa/

121 Retrieved from http://www.transparency.org/

122 Gramm-Leach-Bliley act. Retrieved from http://www.business.ftc.gov/privacy-and-security/gramm-leach-bliley-act

123 Retrieved from https://www.sec.gov/about/laws/soa2002.pdf

124 Health information privacy. Retrieved from http://www.hhs.gov/ocr/privacy/

125 HITECH act enforcement interim final rule. Retrieved from http://www.hhs.gov/ocr/privacy/hipaa/administrative/enforcementrule/hitechenforcementifr.html

126 Bank secrecy act (BSA). Retrieved from http://www.occ.gov/topics/compliance-bsa/bsa/index-bsa.html

127 The USA patriot act: Preserving life and liberty. Retrieved from http://www.justice.gov/archive/ll/highlights.htm

128 Retrieved from https://www.pcisecuritystandards.org/

129 Payment card industry (PCI) data security standard. Retrieved from https://www.pcisecuritystandards.org/documents/pci_dss_v2.pdf

130 About. Retrieved from http://www.treasury.gov/about/organizational-structure/offices/Pages/Office-of-Foreign-Assets-Control.aspx

131 About. Retrieved from http://www.treasury.gov/about/organizational-structure/offices/Pages/Office-of-Foreign-Assets-Control.aspx

132 Protection of personal data. Retrieved from http://ec.europa.eu/justice/data-protection/

133 Complying with the personal information protection and electronic documents act. Retrieved from http://www.priv.gc.ca/resource/fs-fi/02_05_d_16_e.asp

134 Lal Bhnsin, Madan, Corporate Accounting Fraud: A Case Study of Satyam Computers Limited, retrieved from Open Journal of Accounting, 2013, 2, 26-38, http://sx.soi.org/104236/ojacct.2013.22006, Published Online April 2013 (http://www.scirp.ort/journal/ojacct)

135 - 136 http://articles.economictimes.indiatimes.com/2009-05-04/news/28450376_1_bank-accounts-current-account-sfio

137 http://www.sebi.gov.in/cms/sebi_data/attachdocs/1405419346107.pdf, pg 17

138 - 139 http://articles.economictimes.indiatimes.com/2009-05-04/news/28450376_1_bank-accounts-current-account-sfio

140 http://www.slideshare.net/2011barot/satyam-detailed-scam

141 http://www.jokes.net/threeaccountants.htm

142 http://www.quotegarden.com/taxes.html

143 http://www.informationactive.com/index.php?id=419&option=com_content&view=article

144 Mike Jacka http://iaonline.theiia.org

145 Will Rogers http://www.willrogerstoday.com/will_rogers_quotes/quotes.cfm?qID=6 http://www.priv.gc.ca/resource/fs-fi/02_05_d_16_e.asp

www.ingramcontent.com/pod-product-compliance
Lightning Source LLC
Chambersburg PA
CBHW080410300426
44113CB00015B/2467